D0393953

TS-102

**WATER GARDENS
FOR PLANTS AND FISH**

Cover: This exquisitely beautiful and intricately designed garden pond is located at the home of Donald and Betty Ondrak of Phillips, Nebraska.

Photography:
David Alderton, Herbert R. Axelrod, Heiko Bleher, Guido Dingerkus, Jaroslav Elias, Michael Gilroy, T.J. Horeman, Vaclau Laboda, Lilypons Water Gardens, Charles Masters, Robert Mertlich, Vincent Serbin, Paul Stetson, William Tomey, Ruda Zukal, and VanNess Water Gardens.

Illustrations:
Lilypons Water Gardens and John R. Quinn.

© **1988 by T.F.H. Publications, Inc.**

Distributed in the UNITED STATES by T.F.H. Publications, Inc., One T.F.H. Plaza, Neptune City, NJ 07753; in CANADA to the Pet Trade by H & L Pet Supplies Inc., 27 Kingston Crescent, Kitchener, Ontario N2B 2T6; Rolf C. Hagen Ltd., 3225 Sartelon Street, Montreal 382 Quebec; in CANADA to the Book Trade by Macmillan of Canada (A Division of Canada Publishing Corporation), 164 Commander Boulevard, Agincourt, Ontario M1S 3C7; in ENGLAND by T.F.H. Publications Limited, Cliveden House/Priors Way/Bray, Maidenhead, Berkshire SL6 2HP, England; in AUSTRALIA AND THE SOUTH PACIFIC by T.F.H. (Australia) Pty. Ltd., Box 149, Brookvale 2100 N.S.W., Australia; in NEW ZEALAND by Ross Haines & Son, Ltd., 18 Monmouth Street, Grey Lynn, Auckland 2, New Zealand; in SINGAPORE AND MALAYSIA by MPH Distributors (S) Pte., Ltd., 601 Sims Drive, #03/07/21, Singapore 1438; in the PHILIPPINES by Bio-Research, 5 Lippay Street, San Lorenzo Village, Makati Rizal; in SOUTH AFRICA by Multipet Pty. Ltd., 30 Turners Avenue, Durban 4001. Published by T.F.H. Publications, Inc. Manufactured in the United States of America by T.F.H. Publications, Inc.

WATER GARDENS
FOR PLANTS AND FISH

CHARLES B. THOMAS
President, Lilypons Water Gardens

Contents

Foreword

For a century or more the growing of water lilies has delighted American gardeners—that is, a certain number of them. These have sung the praises of the exquisite and opalescent blossoms and emphasized the easy culture in tub, pool, or pond. Unfortunately, they haven't always been believed—about the "ease," I mean, not the beauty. Anyone who has ever seen a water lily blossom readily agrees that it is among the loveliest of flowers.

But pools are hard to build, some argue; pools take up a lot of room; they leak; they get scummy; they're for people with lots of time and money.

But at Lilypons, located near Frederick, Maryland, at Thermal near Palm Springs, California, and at Brookshire, near Houston, Texas, the Thomas family and their associates keep proving these criticisms are unjustified. They have built up a thriving business on aquatic plants and all kinds of materials for water gardening. There are answers to questions about water gardening.

The cost is reasonable, they demonstrate. The guidelines in this book help to keep it simple. And it takes less time to maintain than other forms of gardening.

It should all be in a book, we decided, so that this easiest of gardens could be enjoyed by all

Below: *Healthy fish and succulent foliage!*

Right: *Mother Nature at her best!*

the busiest of people, the ones who don't want to hoe, spray, dust, stake, and trim; the ones who like to sit and enjoy. For them, a clear pool, a few lilies, the flash of fish, and the relaxed attitude are the thing.

This ever-increasing multitude can find in this book what they need to know about easy gardening, that is, water gardening in a tub, in a fiberglass pool, in a PVC–liner pool they can make in a day, or in a quiet pond, if they are lucky enough to have one.

And the dedicated gardener, the enthusiastic one for whom nothing is too much trouble, will find here a thorough discussion not elsewhere available on various aspects of water gardening. Over 150 water lilies and other aquatic plants offered by American water garden specialists are described. Valuable advice is offered as to appearance, culture, propagation, and how to plant the water garden "inside" for balance of life and "outside" for beauty of setting.

Then about fish. If you have a few now, you will soon have a multitude. Once you have read this book, you will find it much less likely that you will lose an expensive favorite through ignorance and you will find it almost impossible to resist further collecting.

This is a grand book, I think,

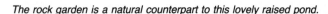

The rock garden is a natural counterpart to this lovely raised pond.

Tropical day blooming lily, Pink Pearl.

simple and delightful in style, sound down to the last detail. When I visited Lilypons, I saw the pools and water lilies in vast numbers and talked at length with the Thomases (actually a husband-and-wife collaboration is responsible for this book). A wonderful American family has developed this aquatic business, and from it has come this delightful book.

Helen Van Pelt Wilson

Helen Van Pelt Wilson is an internationally known editor and speaker who has authored over a dozen gardening books.

Acknowledgment

Grateful acknowledgment is given to all who have contributed to the development of this book, especially to water gardening enthusiasts from far and near. Loving water lilies, accessory aquatic plants, and ornamental pool fish, they have sought answers to their many questions and have provided constant stimulation.

Rolf Nelson and Julia Russu generously gave valuable help in assembling and presenting material. Stephen Myers, Perry Slocum, Lilypons Water Gardens, Stapeley Water Gardens, VanNess Waters, and many water gardeners furnished outstanding photographs, while Anita Nelson and Robert Grove created excellent artwork. Herbert R. Axelrod, Steven Davis, Susan Hesselgesser, Walter Pagels, Perry Slocum, and Kirk Strawn assisted with valuable editing services. Irene Stephenson dedicated many hours typing an error-free manuscript.

Colleagues who gave encouragement, sometimes without realizing it, in addition to those already named, include Norman Bennett, Ray Davies, Robert DeFeo, Bill Heritage, Gordon Ledbetter, John Mirgon, Patrick Nutt, Ernest Page, Frances Perry, Peter Robinson, Peter Slocum, Paul Stetson, Robert Steinbach, Philip Swindells, Joe Tomocik, and Jack Wood.

Finally, I acknowledge my family who made the proper environment so that this book could be written—grandparents Pearl and G. Leicester Thomas who founded Lilypons Water Gardens; parents Virginia and G. L. Thomas, Jr., on whose book this one is based; Maureen and brother George Thomas, III; Frances Thomas and C. Lease

The hardy lily Louise.

The famous French artist Monet glorified water gardens in many of his now-priceless paintings.

Bussard; Annabell Thomas and Carlton Strube; nephew George, IV; daughters Margaret Mary, Virginia, Victoria and Elizabeth; and wife, Sally Snouffer Smith Thomas.

Planning for Your Lily Pond

The blissful serenity of a garden pond located in Kyoto, Japan.

A water lily pond, together with the variety of plants used for decorating its margins, offers a quick and rewarding means of landscaping. A pond of average size can be installed on a weekend, planted, and brought into full bloom in six to eight weeks. What a refreshing sight a pool is for a family in a new home, while they wait for grass and shrubbery to take hold. Or what an attractive focal point it can add to an existing landscape.

THE VERSATILE WATER GARDEN

Water gardens are remarkably varied and adaptive. A water garden may be a farm pond, bigger than a city block, with free growing water lilies scattered over it like a sky full of stars. In the suburbs or city, it may be roughly the size of a living room rug, a sunken affair of fiberglass or PVC (polyvinyl chloride) in the side, front, or back yard; or it may be really tiny, a garden spot taking up no more room than a

14

lawn chair on a condominium balcony—a little living bouquet, all the more beautiful for its small and intimate setting.

A pond in a new landscape can become the center of interest around which the rest of the garden is designed. A new pond placed in an old and beloved garden will bring added magic by reflecting and complementing the flowers already there. And, speaking of magic, I think a shimmering water surface set into a garden is the best possible way to bring a patch of sky down to earth and make it part of the landscape. From a picture window a pool of water lilies is a lovely, refreshing sight and colorful for a long season. By the strategic placement of a pool just outside a window, a gardener can bring the beauty and serenity of waterborne flowers right into the home.

THE TIME, THE EFFORT, THE COST, AND THE VALUE

Expense-wise, water gardening also is widely varied. With a tub, half barrel, or similar container, you can sink a miniature pool in the yard—and plant it with a beautiful water lily—for less than the cost of a night on the town. With only average handiness with tools, you can build a PVC pool big enough for the whole neighborhood to enjoy for as little as an inexpensive TV set costs. It is generally recognized that landscaping is a wise investment that enhances the value of your property.

The biggest effort is getting started. After that, patience is the main requirement for the six to eight weeks following planting while the pool biologically "balances" itself.

The maintenance of a water garden requires less effort than most other forms of gardening.

A gracefully shaped pond located in the Seychelles Islands.

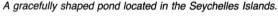

There is no hoeing, no weeding, no over-watering. Given a fair chance, water lilies not only grow and bloom—they thrive. Fortunately, there are few diseases and insect pests that affect them.

I hope I am not dwelling too long on the practical aspects of water lilies. I would want you to consider that, with the possible exception of their wonderful therapeutic value and the satisfying outlet they provide for artistic expression, water lilies have no practical use whatsoever. They are a sheer, out-and-out luxury, existing solely and completely for whatever pleasure their beauty and fragrance may give you. They did, however, inspire Monet, whose paintings of water gardens are now worth millions!

TYPES OF WATER LILIES

Water gardeners think in terms of basic types of water lilies— **hardy** and **tropical.** They are cousins, so to speak, but nobody so far has been able to cross-breed them. The tropicals are divided into two kinds, **day bloomers** and **night bloomers.**

Hardy water lilies are perennials which, in general, propagate themselves with little help from the gardener. You can encourage extra blossoms by adding fertilizer tablets monthly during the growing season. Planted in a large planting container, even though ice covers the pool in winter, they burst into new life from the original rootstock each spring for years.

Hardy water lily blossoms, some no larger than the face of a pocket watch, some as big as an adult's hand, come in many tints and shades except blues and greens. Some of them float upon the water, among their round, smooth-edged leaves. Others, reaching for the sun, especially if crowded or in very shallow water, stand above the water's surface. Many are fragrant.

The "hardies" open their flowers to the sun in the morning and stay open until mid or late afternoon. The blooming season for most is when the afternoon water temperature reaches around 65° F. A single plant produces a flower which opens and closes for three to five days, rests several days, then produces another blossom. This continues until a month or so prior to frost. In frost-free areas, blooming may be reduced during the period of shortest daylight. When you see multiple blooms on a hardy water lily, it usually means that there are daughter plants growing with the original plant in the soil container. Regular feeding and generous-sized soil containers encourage this phenomenon.

Tropicals might be called annuals, for they are treated as annuals by most casual water gardeners. Technically, they are frost-tender perennials. They

The turbulence created by this lovely waterfall aerates the water for the benefit of the ornamental fishes.

17

differ in many ways from the hardies. They typically require more pool space because they grow bigger blossoms and leaves (leaves are frequently scalloped or frilled along their edges). They must be planted outside later than the hardies, when the minimum water temperature is about 70° F. They grow rapidly and their blooms generally continue to appear past the first several frosts. Until then, they often display two or three blossoms at the same time. It is not unusual for a tropical water lily to produce five times as many blossoms per season as a hardy water lily.

Tropicals come in many shades and tints, including reds,

whites, pinks, peaches, greens, yellows, blues, and purples. Tropicals bear their blossoms on stiff, strong stems which carry blooms well above the surface of a pool.

Day Bloomers, Night Bloomers

Tropical water lilies are of two kinds—day bloomers and night bloomers. Day bloomers open their flowers, like the hardy lilies, in the morning, and close them in the late afternoon. Practically every day-blooming tropical has a fine fragrance.

The night-blooming tropicals open their blooms around dusk, and close them around noon the following day. In overcast weather, particularly when the weather is cool, they sometimes refuse to close completely even in the afternoon. This blooming

Gloriosa, a red hardy lily.

pattern enables even the busiest commuter to see them at their best twice a day. Night-blooming tropicals have a heady fragrance.

SELECTING THE SITE

The selection of a site for your pond usually amounts to deciding where it would look best. Actually, however, there are few places where a pool wouldn't look good. Of course,

water lilies that grow with as little direct sunlight as three or four hours daily. Most require at least five or six hours of direct sun. Lotus need at least six hours of direct sun. The more they get, over and above that, the more vigorously they will grow and the better they will bloom. But in any spot where they get a six-hour minimum they

The Susan Hesselgesser pond, a well-established concrete structure.

you want it to blend in naturally with its surroundings. You can be sure that any water feature will become a focal point; water, like fire, attracts attention.

You may select a site that refuses to grow anything. Water lilies don't care what wouldn't grow there before you installed a pool. The major limiting factor to any site is the amount of direct sunlight that falls upon it. Fortunately, there are several

can be depended upon to give satisfaction. The best bloomers for low direct light are some of the tropical day-blooming varieties.

Night-blooming tropicals require as much sunlight as any of the others. Contrary to what seems to be a popular opinion, they draw only moral support from the moon.

CHECKING THE SITE FOR SUNLIGHT

If you are doubtful about a site, check it before you get started. If you have a spot in mind and there are other sun-loving

19

flowers there now, rest assured that water lilies will do as well as or even better.

Stretch out a length of garden hose or clothesline in a design the size and shape you want for your pool, and in the place you have selected. Check the spot several times during a day when the sun is shining, and make allowance for seasonal variation in the sun's path. Then you will know if the site will provide the sun requirements of your water lilies. If the shifting shade of a tree barely edges out the needed amount of sunlight from an otherwise desirable spot, a little judicious pruning may let in enough direct sun to allow you to use your preferred location.

OVERHANGING TREES

A word of warning about trees. I tell water gardeners every year that a water lily planted under a tree is unlikely to bloom. It can produce foliage, but it rarely if ever blooms. At least several times a year people send in letters contradicting my advice. Often the letters are accompanied by a snapshot of a water lily blooming beautifully in a pool in the shade of a spreading tree. All I can say about such occurrences is that these are chance blooms like the dandelions that sometimes come up in February. Believe me, there is no such thing as a "shade" variety of water lily that blooms readily without three or more hours of direct sunlight.

A pool directly under a tree is, therefore, out of the question if water lily blossoms are essential. Even a pool partially under a tree is to be avoided if possible. Leaves and other matter dropped from trees generate gases when they decompose in the pool, and these gases stress—frequently kill—fish. Oak leaves, probably the worst of the lot, give pool water a strong acid content within a few days.

The Dean pool in summer surrounded by a panoply of colorful flowers.

An informal water garden well-stocked with lilies and fish.

COLD WINDS

If it is practical for you (in the snowbelt) to locate your pool beside a building, a line of trees, a hedge, or similar windbreak, so that it is protected from cold winds I would advise you to do so. Shelter from such winds, particularly in early spring, gives water lilies a better chance for an early, healthy start.

DRAINAGE

Another consideration in selecting a site is that of filling and emptying the pool. Filling it entails only the business of running a garden hose out to it from the nearest water tap, and emptying it isn't any more difficult. To empty your pool, simply use a pool pump and tubing to discharge the water, which can benefit nearby plants. Naturally you will want to take care not to put pool water on a neighbor's yard without permission.

NATURAL RUNNING WATER

A natural, flowing body of water usually is too active (and too cool in the snowbelt) for good water lily growth. Water lilies do best in still water warmed by the sun. They sometimes produce foliage in cool water, but they rarely bloom. Flowing water that disturbs the normal round distribution of lily pads is out of the question for growing water lilies.

FORMAL AND INFORMAL POOLS

Esthetically speaking, there are two types of pools—**formal** and **informal.**

A **formal** pool may be practically any classic or regular shape. Obviously it should suit a decorative scheme. Formal pools can be very beautiful, but they should not be attempted if there is too little space. The slightest suggestion of crowding ruins the effect of a formal pool.

The **informal** pool may have just about any kind of outline, although a regular, or at least uncomplicated, shape is likely to be the most pleasing. Through the well-planned arrangement of marginal plants, the informal pool appears to be a work of nature.

There is also the completely natural earth-bottom pond, the spring-fed pond where you have only to plant water lilies to convert the site into a garden. The natural pond is rare and stands in a class by itself. While a chapter on earth-bottom ponds

The simpler and wider the outline, the easier it is to build, the more spacious it appears, the easier it is to maintain, and the magic will be there. Stars, triangles, and contorted shapes should be avoided. By no stretch of the imagination do they fit in with any kind of formal landscape, and it is next to impossible to give them the natural appearance an informal pond should have. Moreover, the more intricate the form, the more

The brick-bordered concrete pond of Dr. and Mrs. R.W. Bailey of Tryon, NC.

is beyond the scope of this book, the most important advice I can give here is to be very careful in selecting which aquatic plants to grow. Lotus, most marginal and submerged plants, and some water lilies spread widely when introduced into such an environment.

Whatever the style of pool decided upon, I strongly recommend a simple shape. It blends easily with the landscape.

difficult it is to build.

Make a sketch of your planned pool on graph paper. Try different shapes to determine its form. Graph paper helps you to determine the maximum amount of pond space for your site. Pools look smaller when they are in the ground than you would think prior to installation. People are often disappointed that their ponds are too small. Very rarely (twice in over 30 years) have I heard complaints about ponds being too big.

Above: *The beauty of this well-stocked pool is augmented by the handsome border and the use of complementary lattice concrete blocks in the background.*

Below: *The background of rockwork enhances the serenity of this lovely garden pond. The small waterfall obviously has not disturbed the stillness of the water to the point where the lilies are affected.*

Above: *Mrs. C.W. Ward.*

Below: *This lovely lily, Patricia Pat, may unfortunately be extinct.*

Above: *Mr. Martin E. Randig.* **Below:** *Golden West.*

Installing Your Pool

BUILDING MATERIALS

Advancements in pool construction have made it easier to install and maintain a water lily pool. Labor intensive and costly concrete pools are rarely installed today. No longer do you have to spend hours pouring concrete and working with reinforcing wire, rebars, and timbers, or waiting for the pool to cure. With a fiberglass pool, the task can be as easy as digging a hole, putting in the pool, and levelling it off. Unlike concrete, which becomes a permanent feature of the landscape, a fiberglass or PVC (polyvinyl chloride) pool is easily moved if you want to change your landscape.

There are many types of materials which may be used for water gardens, including semi-rigid plastic, whiskey barrels, cattle troughs, fiberglass, PVC liners, bathtubs, butyl rubber liners, and ceramic pots. However, in the United States, the favorite flexible material is the PVC liner and the favorite preformed material is the fiberglass pool.

PVC LINERS

PVC liners offer flexibility of design and allow for unlimited size and creativity. You can shape your pond in any design you like, from an outline of the state of Texas to a formal rectangle. PVC should be chosen

Right: *There is an incredible assortment of pond statuary available to create interest in your water garden.*

Below:
There is a fountain for every taste.

26

in thicknesses of 16 to 32 mil (one mil = $\frac{1}{1000}$ of an inch). This offers an estimated life span of 10 to 20 years, depending on the thickness of the PVC and the quality of the installation. Be sure to use a fish grade liner, which is non-toxic to fish and plants. Swimming pool liners often contain chemicals which can remain toxic for extended periods. Most water gardeners say that PVC offers the best balance between price and longevity of any garden pool material available.

If a puncture occurs, it is a simple matter to repair. Clean and dry the area around the puncture. Apply PVC glue to the area and also to a clean piece of excess PVC material saved from when you installed the pool.

Then press the glued patch to the glued puncture area to remedy the problem.

With the use of landscape timbers, a liner pool can be transformed into a rustic above-ground pool. Above-ground pools have the advantage of providing seating space for close inspection of plants and fish. Many people appreciate easier access to the pool. However, in very cold areas, water lilies seem to perform better in in-ground pools than in above-ground pools, and larger above-ground pools seem to produce better results than smaller above-ground pools. The reason for this is that small above-ground pools are more susceptible to sudden and greater temperature changes than are larger above-

This formal garden pond displays all the necessary elements of proportion and symmetry.

K. Molasek's PVC pool presents a lush, tropical look with a wonderful assortment of greenery, colorful fish, and gentle waterfall.

ground pools or in-ground pools, and water lilies seem to prefer that changes in water temperature be very gradual.

PREFORMED FIBERGLASS POOLS

A fiberglass pool is more expensive than a PVC liner of the same size, but it offers distinct advantages. First, fiberglass is the most durable of the pool materials available. Also, it is easy to install and may be used above or below ground. This type of pool may be put on a terrace or inside a greenhouse, and potted plants may then be placed around the pool to mask the edges. Another advantage is

Mary Rose Garrett's informal fiberglass pond displays a delightful collection of plants and natural features.

that fiberglass pools (of good quality fiberglass of one-quarter inch thickness or more) have a life expectancy of over 50 years.

A disadvantage of using preformed fiberglass is that you are limited to the sizes and shapes in which the ponds are made, although they are produced in sizes over 400 gallons in capacity and 13 feet in length.

Use a pond with a black or gray finish, since these colors will appear more natural in your landscape. A black or dark gray pond gives the illusion of greater depth and offers better reflectivity of the sky and the surroundings. Turquoise or blue, on the other hand, would look artificial in your garden.

Installation of Pools

When installing your pool, it is very important that its top edge be level. Any discrepancy will surely be noticed once water has been added, and your pond overflows at one end while the other end stands half a foot above water! Also, a level top edge is essential in attaining a natural looking pond. As construction progresses, be sure to check and recheck the top for levelness.

PVC Liner Installation

Pools that are 18 inches deep are of good average depth for both water lilies and fish. Few water lilies can grow in ponds that are less than 10 inches deep, and few can grow in ponds that offer more than four feet of water over the roots. To

determine the liner size for a rectangular pool that is 18 inches deep, add five feet to the length of the pool and five feet to the width of the pool. (One foot is added for the flap on each side which adds two feet to the length of the liner and two feet to the width of the liner and 18 inches is added for each of the two sloped side walls, which adds another three feet to the length and width of the liner.) For example, a pond 5 feet by 10 feet in size requires a liner that measures 10 feet by 15 feet. A basic rule to remember is that for every six inches you add to a pool's depth, one foot of liner should be added to the liner's length and to the liner's width. Then add two more feet to the liner's length and to the liner's width to allow for a foot of flap.

After you have experience installing liners, you may allow for a six inch flap. This smaller flap provides a larger pool for a given size of liner. But for the neophyte, I recommend the 12 inch flap.

Lay out a rope or hose to the required shape and size of the pond, adjusting until all aspects are satisfactory. Begin digging, but always cut inside the finished outline, to allow for final trimming and shaping. The excavation is started, leaving optional marginal shelves, where and if desired, nine inches wide and nine inches below water level.

Insert short wooden pegs three to four feet apart around the pool, and level the tops using a spirit or line level. *The top edge*

Outline desired shape and size of pool with a rope or hose. Dig, cutting inside the finished outline.

Excavate soil leaving marginal shelves 9 inches wide by 9 inches below water surface. Pool edge should be cut back for edging.

Insert short wooden pegs 3 to 4 feet apart around the pool. Level tops with a spirit level.

of the pond must be level. This is important since the water immediately shows any fault. After final trimming and shaping are complete, the depth and width of marginal shelves should be checked. The sides and base of the excavation must be closely inspected for sharp stones or roots.

Place a cushion of sand one-half inch deep on the bottom of the excavation. Damp sand should then be worked into the sides of the excavation to fill holes and crevices which might have resulted from the removal of stones and such. The finished excavation should be neat and trim, since irregularities will show after the liner is fitted. On stony ground infested with weeds or roots, building grade polyethylene should be underlaid on sides and bottom as an added precaution.

Drape the pool liner loosely into the excavation, leaving an even flap all around. Place smooth rocks on the corners

and, as required, on the sides. Begin filling the pond with water. As the pool fills, ease off the rocks at intervals to allow the liner to fit snugly into the excavation. Creasing is inevitable, but some creases can be removed by hand fitting as the pond fills.

When the pool is full, cut off the surplus lining leaving a 12 inch flap. (After you have experience at this, you may want to work with a six-inch flap.) Temporarily secure the flap with smooth, heavy rocks or by simply pushing four-inch nails through the lining and into the ground to ensure the liner does not slip. If the rim is to be of flagstone, make a series of trial arrangements before you cement the stones in place. Natural-looking stone arrangements are tricky to achieve, and few people hit upon one they really like the first time. Prepare a three-inch base of mortar made with three parts sand to one part cement (add

Complete final trimming and shaping and check depth and width of marginal shelves. Inspect sides and base of excavation closely for sharp stones or roots.

Cushion bottom of excavation with ½-inch depth of damp sand. Work sand into sides of excavation to fill any holes or crevices.

water until you have a workable mixture) reinforced with chicken wire. Press the flagstone in the three-inch base over the liner. When you cement the stones in place, keep the mortar well hidden, for the sight of it will destroy the natural illusion you want to create. If you do slip, cover any exposed mortar with a handful of earth.

If winter temperatures where you live drop below 20° F, follow area practice with reference to mortar proportions, reinforcements, and depth of bed. Extend the rock about two inches over the edge of the pool, to protect the liner from ultraviolet radiation from the sun. This practice and keeping your pond full of water will extend the life of your liner.

If you plan to have a waterfall, build it at the same time as the pond. Use PVC liner as an underlay to prevent leaks. Lay the PVC in a manner so that it returns all water to your pool. Place rocks so that they are

harmonious in the way found in nature.

After the mortar has set for a week, cure it with distilled vinegar or a curing product such as UGL's Drylock Etch. After the mortar has been cured, thoroughly rinse the pond. This precaution can prevent a sudden and potentially disastrous pH change in your pond water.

PREFORMED FIBERGLASS POOL INSTALLATION
Trace around the pool to establish your digging area. Excavate the ground to conform to the shape of the pool. Remove sharp objects. Line the bottom of the hole with one half inch of sand, making a level footing for the pool. Set the preformed pond in the prepared hole and ensure that the rim of the pool is one to two inches above ground level, to prevent runoff water from entering your pool. If you are not concerned with runoff water, then omit the one to two inches of raised rim, which will give your

Drape pool liner loosely with overlap all around. Fill with water.

As pool fills, some creases can be removed by stretching and fitting liner.

When pool is full, cut surplus overlap, leaving a flap of 6 to 12 inches. Temporarily secure this flap with 4-inch nails.

pond a more natural look. If the pool is not level, rework the sand and keep checking with a level until the pool is properly situated.

Put soil or sand around the pond's exterior while running the water into the pond. This helps to equalize pressure on the interior and exterior of the pool. Edge with stones or bricks as described earlier.

POOL RIMS

You can hardly choose a poor finish for the rim of your pool. It is really a matter of personal preference. I would remind you only that a formal pool calls for a formal finish—brick, tile, cut stone, or cast concrete coping. A natural pond calls for a natural finish—which means flagstone or other flat stratified rock, replete with appropriate plants for a more natural appearance. The random shapes of field stones do not lend themselves as well to the construction of a pond rim, and I have never seen a rim so constructed that looked natural.

Decorative tiles or similar ceramic materials chosen as capping for the rim of the pool require special cements, which a tile dealer can supply.

For securing bricks, cast concrete coping, or stone to the pool rim, follow the directions given earlier for PVC liner rims.

SPECIAL EFFECTS FOUNTAINS AND SPOUTS

Everybody who builds a water garden, it seems, has trouble deciding whether or not to put in a fountain.

Edging can now be placed around the pool.

The finished pool.

The established pool.

Use a fountain system that draws its supply of water from the pool itself. Such a fountain may be used with no ill effect at all. Powered by an electrically operated submersible pump, it is efficient and dependable. The whole assembly—base, pump, and fountainhead—is scarcely as large as a loaf of bread. Be sure to use a gentle fountain, which does not disturb water lilies by constantly dropping water directly on the pads or by making waves where lily pads float.

A constant stream of cool, clear water gushing into a pool from an outside source keeps the temperature below that proper for water lily growth. It also keeps the water too free of beneficial bacteria and of microscopic plant life which thrive in a healthy pool, which

Shown are two popular types of fountain.

fish enjoy in addition to the prepared foods they eat.

A fountain provides a beautiful sight indeed, but it looks best in a formal or semi-formal setting. It can look out of place in a natural or rustic pond.

WATERFALLS

If your pond is of rustic or natural design, you may want to add yet another dimension to your garden—the musical sound of falling water. The effect is especially welcome on a hot summer day—both to exhausted humans and to thirsty songbirds.

Power your waterfall with a submersible pump available from your local aquarium store or aquatic plant dealer. To determine the right size pump for your waterfall, look at the pump's gallons per hour rating chart for the appropriate height. Compare this gallons-per-hour figure with the flow you want

Shown is a schematic design of the waterflow in a bilevel pond.

over the waterfall. With 300 gallons per hour, you can expect a half-inch flow over a three-inch wide sill, a quarter-inch deep flow over a six-inch wide sill, or too little water to be significant over a twelve-inch wide sill.

Keep in mind that the rating you want must take into account the vertical and horizontal distance the water travels in the tube between the pump and the discharge. Each 10 feet of horizontal travel in one-half inch inside diameter tubing has roughly the effect of one foot of vertical lift. So if the vertical distance is five feet and the horizontal distance is 10 feet (one foot vertical equivalent), look on the pump's rating chart to see how many gallons per hour it pumps at six feet of vertical lift (the five vertical feet plus the one-foot vertical

equivalent for 10 horizontal feet).

A PVC liner placed under the rocks of a waterfall and raceway catches whatever water might otherwise escape between the rocks. You want all of the recirculating water to return to the pond, so install the liner in such a way that all water it catches returns to the pond.

The bottom stone of a waterfall should overhang the pond so as to provide a sound chamber behind the spot where the falling water hits the pool surface. I can think of no more pleasant and cooling sound on a hot summer evening than that offered by a waterfall.

A number of other interesting effects, such as statues, miniature water wheels, cascades, and even windmills, can be operated by a submersible pump.

Most garden pool pumps have only a six-foot power cord. Safety experts recommend placing power outlets at least six feet away from the edge of a pool. Therefore, I recommend using a pump with at least a 10- or 12-foot cord. They are available. Be sure that the power outlet has a ground fault circuit interrupter, available from aquatic plant specialists and electric goods suppliers. Your electrician can easily install this item.

LIGHTING THE POOL

Among the most spectacular of pool arrangements are the safe, inexpensive, and practical devices with which the water garden can be illuminated at night.

Beautiful surface effects can be obtained by placing bulbs here and there about the rim of the pool, situating them inconspicuously in clumps of border plants, and by beaming spotlights upon the pool from trees or other strategic locations well away from the immediate vicinity. These surface techniques, being both practical and inexpensive, are becoming more popular each season.

A variety of lighting arrangements is now available. Some of the leading electrical laboratories have developed special lights for use in pools. Underwater lights can be easily anchored beneath the surface of the water wherever desired. I recommend using the 12-volt varieties that use a transformer to change household current to a safer low voltage current.

A stern word of caution on illuminating the pool: those companies now manufacturing

Below: *A four-tiered pond ideal for use on a hillside.*

Right: *Natural waterfalls empty into basins, creating multiple ponds.*

submerged lights have developed safe fixtures and proper wiring and connections for them. These devices are the only ones that can be used safely. If you install pool lights, use the proper fixtures, as directed by the manufacturer. Follow local electrical codes. Be sure to use a ground fault circuit interrupter with lights, just as you do with submersible pumps.

A very romantic method of lighting your pond is to use floating candles. They are available in a variety of colors and fragrances from aquatic plant dealers. Water currents cause them to drift here and there around your pond, creating a marvelous effect. Floating candles when used normally

Diagram of elaborate waterfall, pond, and island arrangement.

have never, in my experience, caused damage to any pond, but do remember to keep flames away from any flexible liner.

POOLS FROM TUBS, TANKS, AND KETTLES

Wooden tubs and half barrels sunk into the ground fit beautifully into small spaces and provide a pleasant focal point in the yard. But remember that **new** wood can be injurious to fish, and a certain amount of aging is necessary. A receptacle that has been out in the weather through the winter should do nicely as is. A whiskey barrel should not be used until you can no longer smell a trace of its former contents.

However, if you can't wait, line it with ordinary black polyethylene or fish grade PVC. Thumbtacks or staples placed

Water lilies planted in a tub. This photo proves that you need not have an abundance of space to enjoy the pleasures of water gardening.

around the top interior will keep the material in position. After the first season, the wood should be sufficiently aged so that you may remove the liner.

Wooden receptacles which have ever contained a toxic substance are out of the question. No amount of treatment can completely cleanse the wood, and neither flower nor fish will do well in containers so tainted.

Steel tanks, iron kettles, and old bathtubs can be used quite effectively as sunken miniature pools. Be sure to coat the inside of iron containers with a good rubber-base paint, which can be purchased from a water lily dealer. For the tanks and kettles, it is a protective measure, since their unpainted surfaces can rust and discolor the water. Paint does not adhere to smooth bathtub porcelain. However, some water gardeners have reported success in painting these surfaces with thick, fast

setting roofing cement.

A good rule to follow in any doubtful situation with a new pond is to experiment by first stocking inexpensive fish. If these are still lively after a couple of weeks, then you may try more delicate stock. I recommend using a water quality test kit so you can scientifically measure for several key components of water quality. These kits are available from your aquarium store or aquatic plant dealer.

MINIATURE POOLS

Various new or used receptacles can be adapted prettily to the construction of sunken miniature pools. A few prerequisites apply to all of them, however, regardless of their shape or material.

Stock your miniature pool with a water lily or miniature lotus, a few bunches of submerged plants, and a vertical accent bog plant, such as iris. Add one or two pairs of snails (sanitation department) and a pair of goldfish to eat mosquito larvae. Good hardy water lilies for small pools include Helvola, Chromatella, or Fabiola. Or you may select from tropicals such as Charles Thomas, Panama Pacific, Colorata, or Dauben. Excellent choices for lotus varieties include Momo Botan Minima and Tulip Lotus.

Safe Pools For Children

A number of water gardeners have written me asking if there is any way of constructing an attractive pool around which toddling children can play in safety. Happily, there are a couple of ideas which I can suggest for your consideration.

The Raised Pool

One such idea is the raised pool. A popular style uses a frame made of landscape timbers with a PVC pool liner on the inside. Such pools can rest entirely on top of the ground, or they may be sunken part way.

While it is generally true that water lilies planted in a tub or similar container and left above ground do not bloom as well, this does not apply to raised pools larger than a card table. The water mass in pools this big or bigger is enough to ensure a daily temperature about the same as for an in-ground pool. Still, the water temperature is somewhat higher in summer and somewhat colder in winter. Fish and water lilies do as well in large raised pools as they do anywhere else. In the snowbelt, you need to provide an indoor or in-ground sanctuary for your above-ground pool inhabitants, if

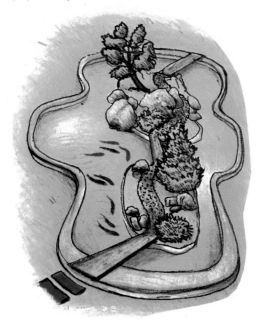

Large pond sectioned for optimal viewing of fish.

The exquisite Mirgon pool in Denver, Colorado.

they are to survive winter's
freezing weather.

The Hidden Screen
The addition of a device which
can be quickly fashioned and
made to fit into any pool of
regular shape provides even
more safety. With three-quarter-
inch pipe, construct a frame
which fits as a snug rim around
the inside of the pool. Cover this
framework with strong
galvanized wire fencing (four- or
five-inch mesh). Screw hooks or
brackets into the framework four
inches below the water line. Test
it carefully to see if it supports
the weight of an adult. Check it
periodically to make sure it is still
structurally sound.

Water lilies and other aquatics
will grow freely through the
fencing, and goldfish do not
seem to notice it at all. The
fencing cannot be seen from any
point except directly above the
pool. And, best of all, a child

accidentally tumbling into the
pool tumbles into only a few
inches of water.

If your toddlers are particularly
rambunctious and you want to
play doubly safe, combine both
approaches and build a raised
pool with the protective
framework included within it.

Local Regulations
Some jurisdictions regulate pool
installation. The usual
requirement is that a pond over
a certain depth, typically 18
inches, be fenced. This implies
that pools under 18 inches in
depth are considered safer than
deeper ones. Most water
gardeners prefer a pond depth in
the 15 inch to 18 inch range. If
you are in doubt about
regulations in your area, I
recommend checking with your
local authorities prior to
beginning pool construction.

William C. Uber, a tropical day bloomer.

Trail Blazer, a tropical day bloomer.

Hardy Water Lilies

Hardy water lilies bloom in the daytime. They open around nine a.m. and close around three p.m. for three to five consecutive days. Assuming a single crown (growing point), several days usually pass before the next bud reaches the water surface. As a rule, the flowers float, although some varieties thrust them above the surface of the water, especially if the plants are crowded or in very shallow water. Hardies grow throughout the North Temperate Zone and there are even some growing in Alaska. They vary in color, spread, light requirements, and fragrance.

Froebeli, a hardy water lily.

Above: *Sulphurea, a hardy water lily.*

Right: *Attraction, a hardy water lily.*

Of all the water lilies, a group of hardies called **changeables** is one of the most fascinating. A changeable water lily is just that. Its bud unfolds with a bloom of one color. Before the end of the first day, the hue of the flower begins to change to another color and then yet another. So, in three successive days of blooming, the flower presents three distinct hues. Catalogs frequently list these as sunset, autumn, or apricot shades.

HARDY WHITE LILIES

Gladstone is a robust plant that requires full sun, has a slight fragrance, and can be grown in water up to 3 feet deep.

Gonnere also requires full sun. It has a very double flower with pure white petals. Gonnere is a good cut flower, has no fragrance, and is often called Snowball. **Hermine** blossoms abundantly over a long season, has a slight fragrance and can be grown in partial or full sun.

Marliac Albida is a fragrant, prolific bloomer, requires full sun, and is good in small ponds.

Odorata gigantea has large cup-shaped flowers and is very fragrant. This plant requires full sun, and is recommended only for earth bottom ponds where spreading is desired to a depth of 5 to 6 feet. Start at 1 to 2 feet of depth and allow to spread. Not recommended for growing in soil containers in garden pools.

Queen of Whites has broad, clear white petals that form outstanding cup-shaped flowers. It has a slight fragrance and requires full sun. **Virginalis** is a slightly fragrant excellent bloomer, requires full sun, and grows in water up to 3 feet deep.

Virginia has large, nearly double flowers, a long season, and can be grown in partial or full sun. No fragrance.

Gladstone, Gonnere, Odorata gigantea, Queen of Whites, Virginialis, and Virginia have a spread of 6 to 12 plus square feet. Hermine has a spread of 1 to 6 square feet. Marliac albida has a spread of 6 to 12 square feet. As with all lilies spread can

Top: *Chromatella.*
Center: *Gloriosa bud.*
Bottom: *Marliac Albida.*
All are hardy.

vary somewhat based on container size, fertility of the soil, stillness of the water, and light.

HARDY PINK LILIES

Fabiola, with a slight fragrance, produces several flowers at a time over a long season. This plant prefers full sun and is a good beginner lily. **Firecrest** prefers full sun and has clear pink flowers with a sharp sweet fragrance. Stamens are a blend of orange, yellow, and red, creating a fire effect. Slightly fragrant, **Hollandia** has large, double flowers borne in profusion. This sun-loving lily is a good cut flower. **Joanne Pring** is a small plant with dark pink flowers to 2 inches. It requires full sun and is excellent for tubs and other small pools. No fragrance. **Marliac Carnea**, a fragrant lily, is good for cut flowers. Grows well in shallow or deep pools to 36 inches. Requires full or partial sun. Fragrant, with spotted rose pink petals and white sepals, **Masaniello** thrives in full or partial sun. The lovely **Mrs. C.W. Thomas** lily has large, very fragrant, shell pink flowers and does well in full sun. **Pearl of the Pool** has very cup-shaped, fragrant, rich pink flowers and requires full sun. **Pink Opal** is fragrant with dark pink flowers with bronze-hued leaves. Requires full sun. **Pink Sensation** has large, fragrant, light pink flowers which remain open late into the afternoon. Full sun. **Rose Arey** will spread in earthen ponds, and also does well planted in soil containers in garden pools. Fragrant, requiring

49

full sun, this lily has sharply pointed petals. Good in small pools. Takes an extra six weeks to establish. **Rose Arey Hybrid** is one of the first lilies to bloom in spring. Requires full sun. The fragrant, light to medium pink flowers open in early morning. **Rosy Morn** produces large flowers on a medium-size plant and requires full sun. The

of the soil, stillness of the water, and light. Fabiola, Marliac Carnea, and Rose Arey spread 3 to 12 square feet. Firecrest, Masaniello, Pearl of the Pool, Pink Opal, Pink Sensation, and Rosy Morn have a spread of 6 to 12 square feet. Hollandia, Mrs. C.W. Thomas, and Rose Arey Hybrid have a spread of 6 to 12 plus square feet.

Virginalis, a hardy lily.

fragrant, erect, two-tone rosy pink petals make for a good cut flower.

Mrs. C.W. Thomas and Pearl of the Pool are recommended only for earth bottom ponds where spreading is desired to a depth of 5 to 6 feet. Start them in water 12 to 18 inches deep. Spread can vary somewhat based on container size, fertility

HARDY YELLOW LILIES

Charlene Strawn holds its fragrant flowers well above the water surface. It has a long season and thrives in full or partial sun. **Chromatella** does well in full or partial sun. This lily has a long season and very mottled blooms. Superb plant for tubs and small pools. No fragrance. **Helvola** is a true pygmy lily. Leaves are slightly

Above: *Fabiola, a hardy lily.*

Right: *Firecrest, a hardy lily.*

Sunrise.

mottled. Flower is the size of a 50¢ piece. Does well in either full or partial sun. **Sulphurea** is a fragrant lily, good for small pools. Flowers are held slightly above the surface. Leaves are slightly mottled. Does well in full or partial sun. **Sunrise** has a slight fragrance and large, yellow flowers borne over a long season. Flowers remain open later in the afternoon than other hardies.

Charlene Strawn has a spread of 6 to 12 square feet. Chromatella and Sulphurea spread 3 to 12 square feet. Helvola spreads 1 to 2 square feet. Sunrise spreads 12 plus square feet. Spread can vary somewhat based on container size, fertility of the soil, stillness of the water, and light.

HARDY RED LILIES
Attraction is a classical deep red lily with a slight fragrance. It blooms freely in water up to 3 feet deep. Does well in full or partial sun. **Ellisiana** is a superb lily for small pools and tubs. Flowers have many dark red petals. Full sun. No fragrance. **Escarboucle** has fragrant brilliant red flowers with somewhat pointed petals. Full sun. **Flammea** has a slight fragrance, deep red flowers flecked with white and produced over a long season. Good cut flower. Full sun. **Froebeli** is a dark red lily, excellent for small pond or tub. Blossoms take southern heat over a long season. Full sun. No fragrance. **Gloriosa** does well in full or partial sun. The fragrant flowers

remain open later in the afternoon than most hardies. Good in tubs and small ponds. **James Brydon** is a superb choice for all pond situations. The fragrant, cup-shaped flowers are borne in profusion on a plant which is at home in tub garden or large pool. Full or partial sun. **Sirius** has large, slightly fragrant, vermillion flowers with orange stamens. The attractive green foliage is flecked with maroon splotches. Does well in full or partial sun. **Splendida** is a good, slightly fragrant, medium-sized plant with strawberry red flowers. Full sun. **Sultan** is a prolific bloomer with slightly fragrant, cherry red flowers. A good grower. Full sun. **William Falconer** has very dark red flowers with maroon foliage early

in the season changing to green. Full sun. No fragrance.

Special note to sunbelt gardeners: Some of these water lilies do not perform well when the temperature exceeds 95°F for a prolonged period. Extreme summer heat causes their flowers to burn and foliage production to decrease. While good results are obtained in the spring and fall, you may wish to avoid planting the red varieties Ellisiana and William Falconer.

Froebeli's spread is 3 to 6 square feet. Ellisiana and Gloriosa spread 3 to 12 square feet. Flammea, James Brydon, Splendida, Sultan, and William Falconer spread 6 to 12 square feet. Attraction, Escarboucle, and Sirius spread 6 to 12 plus square feet. Spread can vary

William Falconer.

somewhat based on container size, fertility of the soil, stillness of the water, and light.

CHANGEABLE LILIES

Comanche presents a nearly yellow flower upon first opening, passing to a coppery bronze color as it matures. The mature leaves are speckled. A good, slightly fragrant cut flower. Comanche will do well in full or partial sun. **Graziella** is a slightly fragrant lily with strongly variegated foliage. Excellent in shallower pools and tubs. Full or partial sun. **Paul Hariot** is a small, fragrant plant with flowers up to 4 inches across. Foliage is nicely mottled. Excellent in tubs and small ponds. Good cut flower. Full or partial sun.

Comanche has a spread of 6 to 12 square feet. Graziella spreads 2 to 6 square feet. Paul Hariot spreads 2 to 8 square feet. Spread can vary somewhat based on container size, fertility of the soil, stillness of the water, and light.

Gloriosa, a hardy lily.

Above: *Comanche, a hardy lily.*   **Below:** *Attraction, a hardy lily.*

Tropical Water Lilies

Tropical water lilies do everything on a grander scale than the hardies. They grow wider and taller, and their flowers occur in a greater range of colors. Their blooming habits are more varied, many of them blooming in daytime, the rest opening at night. Day bloomers have a sweet fragrance while night bloomers have a medicinal fragrance. Both carry their blooms aloft, well above the surface of the water. Long, strong stems make most of them, day bloomers in particular, excellent for cutting.

There are more species of tropicals than of hardies, and they hybridize more readily, which has resulted in a tremendous number of varieties. (Incidentally, I use the terms hybrid and variety

Panama Pacific.

Sir Galahad, a tropical night bloomer.

interchangeably.)

The foliage of most tropicals is spreading and luxurious, sometimes toothed and crimped or fluted at the edge. Most of them require more pool or pond space, half again to twice as much as the hardies.

In Hawaii, and in those other fortunate areas of the United States which are never hit by frosts, tropicals are not limited to seasonal life spans. They live continually, year after year, and bloom the year around, with only brief rest periods. Dauben survives cold better than other tropicals; nevertheless, it is killed by repeated frosts.

As with hardy water lilies, tropical water lilies vary in flower color, spread, and sunlight requirements. All have a fragrance, and there is considerable variation in their foliage.

VIVIPAROUS WATER LILIES

One species and several hybrids of day-blooming tropical water lilies have a very interesting characteristic. They are viviparous, that is, they bear their young alive, in the form of miniature plants and blooms which sprout from an umbilicus at the center of mature leaves.

TROPICAL DAY BLOOMERS

Marian Strawn has large, stately, white blooms that hold well above water surface. Foliage is speckled. This lily does well in full or partial sun. **White Delight** has speckled foliage and requires full sun. This is a very dynamic lily with large, 12-inch, creamy white-tinted blossoms. Occasionally shows soft pink on the petal tips. **Aviator Pring** has deep yellow flowers held well above the water's surface. It has mottled foliage and requires full sun. **St. Louis** produces large, 6- to 8-inch, soft yellow flowers. This lily does well in full or partial sun and has speckled foliage. **Yellow Dazzler** has speckled foliage, requires full sun, and the strong yellow flowers remain open until dusk. **Albert Greenberg** has strongly mottled foliage, and can be grown in full or partial sun. This robust, rosy-yellow plant continues blooming well past early frost. **Golden West** thrives in full or partial sun, has mottled foliage, and salmon pink flowers upon opening, deepening to apricot.

Afterglow, a salmon pink tropical day bloomer.

St. Louis, a tropical day bloomer.

Director Moore produces many 4- to 8-inch speckled leaves and often clusters of purple flowers. Full or partial sun. **Panama Pacific** is a purple lily suited to all pond situations from tubs to large public ponds. It has speckled foliage and is quite viviparous late in the season. Viviparous is a term indicating this water lily is capable of producing a plantlet on the upper leaf surface. Full or partial sun.

Marian Strawn spreads 1 to 12 square feet. Golden West and Director Moore spread 6 to 12

square feet. Panama Pacific spreads 1 to 12 plus square feet. White Delight, Aviator Pring, St. Louis, Yellow Dazzler, and Albert Greenburg spread 6 to 12 plus square feet. Spread can vary somewhat based on container size, fertility of the soil, stillness of water, and light.

PINK DAY BLOOMERS
Evelyn Randig has strongly mottled, beautifully variegated foliage offsetting deep magenta flowers. Full sun. **General Pershing** blooms well late in season. The flowers open in

59

White Delight, tropical day bloomer.

early morning and close at dusk. Mottled foliage. **Pink Capensis** is easy to grow, full sun. This is a prolific bloomer with green or speckled leaves. **Pink Perfection**, strongly mottled foliage, full or partial sun. Strong blooming, rose pink lily. Performs well in shallow or deep ponds. **Pink Platter** profusely produces large, medium pink flowers. Occasionally produces viviparous shoots. Full sun. Speckled foliage. **Pink Star** has green foliage with star-shaped flowers often held 12 inches above the water surface. Full sun.

All of the above lilies spread 6 to 12 plus square feet.

BLUE DAY BLOOMERS

Blue Beauty is a profuse bloomer. An excellent plant for almost all ponds. Full sun. Speckled foliage. **Blue Capensis** does well in shallow or deep ponds. Speckled green foliage. Full sun. **Blue Star** has star-shaped flowers held high above the water surface. Best suited to larger ponds. Green foliage. Full sun. **Bob Trickett** has large, clear blue flowers with a yellow center and green foliage. Full sun. **Charles Thomas** produces periwinkle flowers consistently over a long season with many viviparous shoots late in season. Does well in full or partial sun. Mottled foliage. **Colorata** has abundant wisteria blue flowers and green foliage. This pygmy variety is excellent for tubs even

Day blooming tropical lily—King of the Blues.

Day blooming tropical lily—Yellow Dazzler. The butterfly is a Black Swallowtail.

Night blooming tropical lily—Maroon Beauty.

Blue Star, a tropical day bloomer.

with just 6 inches of water over the plant. Full or partial sun. **Dauben** is the best lily for lower light areas. Highly viviparous. Often has several flowers open at once. Green or speckled leaves. **Leopardess** has clear medium blue flowers which are beautifully contrasted with strongly mottled leaves. Full or partial sun. **Margaret Mary** is a medium-sized plant in pond situations. Adapts to a 2-quart pot. Slightly viviparous with green foliage. Full or partial sun. **Mrs. Martin E. Randig** adapts to tub gardening or large ponds. Very viviparous with green foliage. Full or partial sun.

Pamela has mottled leaves and rich blue flowers produced over a long season. Full sun. **Robert Strawn** has lavender blue flowers held well above the water's surface. Full or partial sun. Green or speckled foliage.

Colorata spreads 1 to 6 square feet. Pamela, Margaret Mary, and Blue Capensis spread 6 to 12 square feet. Blue Star and Bob Trickett spread 12 plus square feet. Charles Thomas, Dauben, and Robert Strawn spread 1 to 12 square feet. Leopardess and Blue Beauty spread 6 to 12 plus square feet. Mrs. Martin E. Randig spreads 1 to 12 plus square feet.

Above: *Blue Beauty.*　　**Below:** *Blue Capensis.*

63

NIGHT BLOOMING TROPICAL LILIES

Emily Grant Hutchings is a superb bloomer often producing rose/red clustered flowers. Foliage has a bronze cast. Full or partial sun. **H.C. Haarstick** is a large rose/red lily producing flowers with a tinge of purple at the base of the petals. Full sun. Bronze cast foliage. **Maroon Beauty** produces maroon red flowers borne on a plant with bronze red foliage. Full sun. **Red Flare** has spectacular flowers with dark red petals and deep maroon stamens. Foliage is red tinged. Full sun. **Mrs. George C. Hitchcock** produces excellent, large pink flowers that continue late into the season. Foliage is maroon. **Texas Shell Pink** is a great-blooming, light pink lily with green foliage. Full or partial

Blue Star.

Texas Shell Pink, night bloomer.

sun. **Juno** produces large, pure white flowers and green foliage. Grows well in water from 10 to 36 inches deep. Full or partial sun. **Wood's White Knight** is good for medium to large ponds. Very prolific. White flowers with green foliage. Full or partial sun.

H.C. Haarstick spreads 12 plus square feet. Emily G. Hutchings, Maroon Beauty, Mrs. George C. Hitchcock, Texas Shell Pink, Juno, and Wood's White Knight spread 6 to 12 plus square feet.

Erect night-blooming lilies holding their heads well above the water.

Planting the Pool

NUMBER OF WATER LILIES FOR A POOL

The best advice I can give you in the interest of an attractive pool is: **Do not crowd it.** Many new water gardeners tend to overdo planting. So here is a rule of thumb that may help. Cover no more than two thirds of the pool surface with water lilies. Leave room for some submerged, floating, and border aquatics. You also will want some free, clear water space.

Figure your square footage of water surface. An 8- by 10-foot pool, for example, gives you 80 square feet. Now, remember that most water lilies fall into one of three size classifications. Extensive growers cover 12 square feet or more when mature; medium growers cover 6 to 12 square feet; small growers confine themselves to 6 square feet or less.

So, for your 8- by 10-foot pool, select only enough water lilies to cover 54 square feet or thereabouts. This will give you room for more plants than you may imagine—four extensive

Plant containers for the pond. Notice underwater growth pattern of the water lily.

Nymphaea nouchali *growing wild in Sri Lanka.*

growers, six medium growers, or as many as ten small growers. However, if your pool is small, you may prefer to sacrifice some of the free water surface, so that you can enjoy an extra water lily. With larger pools you may find that half coverage is generous enough. This is only a general guide to help beginners. Your preferences and experiences may vary, and you then plan future stocking accordingly.

PLANTING ON THE POOL FLOOR
Water lilies and most other ornamental aquatic plants have roots which grow in soil. You could cover the bottom of your pool with five or six inches of soil for growing your water plants; however, **I don't recommend it.** First, this would require extra work in moving a lot of soil. Second, the pond would likely become cloudy, since it would contain a considerable quantity of mud. Third, the more vigorous plants would crowd out the less vigorous ones. Also, I do not recommend putting a layer of sand or gravel on the bottom of your pool, since the addition of such a layer would make cleaning your pool much more difficult.

When overcrowded, the leaves of water lilies rise above the surface of the water seeking sunlight.

PLANTING IN SOIL CONTAINERS

Soil containers make the work far easier. With a plastic pan, pail, or tub, you can work where you choose, setting the receptacles into place in the pond where you choose. Then you can rearrange them as often as you like, without damage to the plants. You will also find it a simple matter to take up a particular lily, should you want to examine it or cut a rootstock from it for a friend.

Controlling Growth

Soil containers also offer the advantage of controlling growth. Water lilies, through their many varieties, are much like people. Some are shy and retiring. Some are bold and ambitious. The strong will crowd out the weak in short order if they are not restrained, so care must be taken. The most practical way of keeping a strong, prolific water lily in check is by planting it in a container, so that you can thus prevent over-zealous spreading. For a weaker variety, you can keep soil and fertilizer in one spot, where roots will have exclusive access to it.

Example of potted irises on marginal shelf.

Regulating Depth

The ideal water depth for lilies ranges from three to six inches, for some varieties when very young, to two to three feet for others. I suggest an 8 to 18 inch range for water depth (subject to possible local codes) over the soil for water lilies and lotus.

Use the suggested ranges unless you have what appears to be a very young short-stemmed plant which might drown if planted as recommended for adult plants. For example, if the young plant has foliage which was exposed to the atmosphere when you bought it, then you will want to plant it in shallow enough depths so that its leaves would still reach to the atmosphere.

A water lily—particularly a young tropical plant—does far better if, in early stages of growth after being transplanted, it passes through increasing depths in progressive stages. This can be achieved quite easily. Simply prop up the planting pan at the desired height with bricks. As the season moves on and growth progresses, you can increase the depth gradually by pulling out one layer of bricks at a time. Make sure that two or three pads are able to float on the water's surface after lowering the plant to each new depth.

PLANTING PANS, BUCKETS, TUBS

Water lilies can be planted in much the same kind of container you use for your porch flowers—with one exception. Because of the tremendous growth they make in a season, water lilies require quite a bit more soil and fertilizer. Feed water lilies and lotus once a month during the growing season. This encourages them to produce more blossoms.

At this point, I think it would be proper to mention that the tremendous blooms pictured in water lily catalogs are not exaggerations. Flowers can attain the near unbelievable size that dealers claim, provided plants are set out and fed according to directions. Give them plenty of direct sunlight, plenty of heavy top soil, and the proper amount of fertilizer.

The most popular soil container for water lilies in the typical garden pond is about 12" across and 6" deep. This is the minimum suggested size container for most water lilies. Anything larger than two feet by two feet by 10" deep is a waste of space in most water gardens. As for strength, any container qualifies as long as it will hold together well enough for you to move it about and take it out of

Typical pot for water lily planting.

Some submerged varieties require relatively shallow water. Raise pot with bricks to achieve correct water depth.

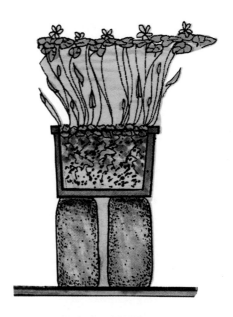

the pool occasionally. There is no need for a hole in the container, since the soil drainage will be saturated with water. I recommend using the plastic pans, pails, and tubs that are available from water gardening dealers.

Wooden tubs, buckets, and half barrels are fine, so long as they are clean and have no residue of any substance toxic to fish, scavengers or aquatic plants. Whiskey barrels are safe to use after the smell of alcohol is gone.

Metal tubs, buckets, and similar containers also do well, but don't use containers made of copper. An old-fashioned dishpan, the kind which turns up at country auctions, is excellent.

Any water lily dealer can furnish you with, or tell you where to find, planting pans, tubs, and buckets. It is also a simple matter to nail together your own containers. Make planting boxes of used lumber, if possible. New woods can exude a "flavor" that is harmful to goldfish.

Aged cypress makes excellent long-lived wooden containers. Avoid using redwood since it discolors the water with an exudation that stunts water lilies. If the boxes that you have constructed have wide cracks, line them with polyethylene to prevent the soil from washing out.

Soil

It is important to start with proper soil. I recommend heavy garden top soil; loam is great. You need a heavy soil so it will stay in place in your soil container. Soil that sticks together when wet is best.

Some professional growers

71

advocate using swamp or river muck, and they are successful. Besides, don't water lilies exist naturally in muck? Nevertheless, I don't recommend it. It's too much trouble for most gardeners to obtain and handle, there's danger of introducing nuisance aquatic plant seeds, and too few people report favorable experience.

If you don't have the recommended heavy garden top soil, use (temporarily) whatever heavy top soil you do have. Even sandy top soil can be used. Clay may comprise up to 25% of the soil, but only so long as you regularly fertilize your lilies and lotus. They will benefit from the needed nutrients and you can expect results with less than the preferred soil. Later, re-pot your water lilies in heavy garden top soil. Lotus, of course, should be transplanted in spring, when the tubers are sprouting their first pads.

Lotus plants do well in soil with a composition of up to 25% clay. With lotus, of course, you should only re-pot during the spring, when the rootstock is in tuber form. Runners, which develop around the same time that aerial leaves are displayed, have a poor transplant survival rate.

Soil for water lilies and lotus should be free of peat moss and rotted wood. Do not use commercial potting soil. It is not designed for underwater use. It is very light and tends to float to the surface. If you do not have top soil, obtain some from a nursery or garden center.

Fertilizers

Do not use fresh manure of any kind, as it sours whatever soil it is put into, discolors pool water to a point of unsightliness, and promotes a quick and excess growth of green algae.

I recommend using fertilizer tablets which are available from aquatic nurseries, garden centers, and nurseries that deal in aquatic materials. Follow the directions, which typically suggest monthly feeding during the growing season.

HARDY ROOTSTOCKS

Hardy rootstocks are of four kinds. Those offspring of the native American white water lily, *(Nymphaea odorata),* have long, earth-colored, fleshy rhizomes. Dealers furnish a five- to six-inch section that is an inch or so in diameter. "Eyes," which occur here and there along the rhizome, can develop into new plants.

Rootstocks of the magnolia water lily hybrids *(Nymphaea tuberosa)* are of similar size and shape, but their rhizomes are less dense and their daughter plantlets are rather loosely attached. Both types propagate by sending up new plants from their rhizomes. If left alone for years, rhizomes can grow several feet in length. In your pool, rhizomes can lengthen enough in a year or two for you to cut off sections which can develop into nice new plants for yourself or for friends.

By damming a natural channel, one is able to create a wonderful pond. Indigenous plants accent pond margins.

Nuphar advena *rootstock*.

Filling your pond with the hose raised above water provides additional aeration for the benefit of plant and animal alike.

Rootstocks of the Marliac hybrids are of two kinds. One develops a pineapple-like form, which is crowned by a single growing point. As the mass grows larger and larger, it produces eyes which can generate new water lilies. Comanche, other changeables, and Chrometella are examples. Gladstone and most red hardies are examples of the elongated, black Marliac rootstock. Elongated Marliac rhizomes produce fewer eyes than *odorata* and *tuberosa* rhizomes, while pineapple-like Marliac rootstock produces the most eyes of the four forms. They tend to stay in a clump rather than travel. This makes them more desirable for earth-bottom ponds where only limited coverage is desired. Staying in clumps is an advantage when growing in soil containers too. This means that it will take longer to become rootbound, longer before re-potting is needed.

WHEN TO PLANT

When you prepare to plant your water lilies, it is a good idea to have soil, fertilizer, and containers ready. Aquatic nurseries will not send plants to you until the weather in your particular area is safe for setting them out. Growth should already have started when you receive your plants. Plant as soon as possible after arrival, as a safeguard against drying out, which might check new growth. Also, avoid exposure to sun and wind, since even five minutes of it can be harmful. If you cannot plant immediately, open the box or package anyway, and examine the contents. Make sure the packing material is moist. Keep your plants in a plastic bag in the shade. Avoid freezing temperatures, as well as those over 80 ° F.

The earliest week you can receive your order of hardy water lilies will be dependent upon your local environment. The afternoon water temperature should be 50°F or higher.

Time of shipment for hardy water lilies also depends on the judgment of your dealer. If there has been a late spring, and summer is slow in getting under way, your dealer may not ship until well into spring, as a concession to human comfort. Neither the person pulling up your lily nor you when planting it would enjoy working with hands made numb by cold water. Late frost will not harm your newly planted hardy water lilies.

Dealers ship tropical water lilies with plant safety in mind. The minimum water temperature should be about 70°F. By that time your hardies may be well started, but tropicals make up for their late arrival with a long season.

PLANTING HARDY WATER LILIES

Planting is simplicity itself. I recommend preparing the planting at poolside. Fill your soil

Comanche water lily, compare color with photo on right.

container two-thirds to three-fourths full of damp heavy garden top soil. If you prefer to work with dry soil, fine. Saturate it with water as soon as you have completed the planting. Next, place the elongated-type rootstock *odorata, tuberosa,* or elongated shaped Marliac types on a 30° angle, the old part an inch or two below the surface of the soil, with the growing tip extending above the soil, or place the pineapple-shaped Marliac rootstock vertically (or nearly so) with the crown (growing point) just barely out of the soil. To do this, hold the rootstock in one hand while maneuvering soil with the other. First, make something of a hole for the lower end of the

Comanche, a changeable orange. This lily is still in full blossoms even though it is so late in the season that the autumn leaves have begun to fall.

rootstock, and then add soil so that the crown is just barely out of the soil. Press the soil firmly around the rhizome. The crown may be only a sprout, or it may include developing flower and leaf stems that are a few inches long, or even up to several feet in length. Regardless of its appearance, it is of utmost importance that the crown is exposed to the water, and is not covered with soil, sand or gravel.

Add water lily fertilizer tablets as recommended on the container label. Then cover the soil surface in the planting container with gravel, but keep it away from the growing point. The gravel layer keeps fish from disturbing the soil and thus clouding the pool. Next, gently pour water from your pond into the newly planted soil container until water has displaced the air in the soil. This prevents a bubbling effect which would make your water cloudy and could dislodge the newly planted water lily. Carefully place the container in the pool.

If the stems of the lily you are planting are fairly well developed, set the container in the pool so that up to 18 inches of water covers the crown. If some leaves lack an inch or so of reaching the water's surface, don't worry about them. They will adjust themselves to their water depth within a few days. I do not recommend having less than six inches of water over the soil.

If growth has just begun, prop up the container so that six inches of water covers the crown. This will allow the warmth of the sun to easily penetrate the water and to stimulate growth. After a week or so, as stems and leaves develop rapidly, the plant can be placed at the proper depth. The important thing to remember is that at least one or two pads should float so that they can breathe.

Watch the level of the water after planting either hardies or tropicals. If the water lowers appreciably, the stems will curl in an attempt to keep their buds under water until they are ready to open. Blooming will more readily occur if the plants are placed at their proper, comfortable level.

PLANTING TROPICAL WATER LILIES

Planting tropicals differs only a little from the approach used for the hardies, but the differences are important. As indicated previously, they should be set out when the water in the pool maintains a minimum temperature of about 70° F. Tropicals can be planted in shallower water than can the hardies. They produce nicely with 6 to 12 inches of water above their crowns.

Tropicals produce more foliage and more flowers than hardies, and therefore need more food. Use the same kind of soil as for the hardies, but feed them twice a month. Up to a point, the tropicals will grow larger as you grow them in larger containers, but regardless of container size, allow them more

surface area than you would for the hardies.

Tropical water lilies are sent from the dealer as growing plants, not as sprouted rootstock only. Their roots are encased in moist packing material. Be careful to protect tropicals from wind and sun before they are placed in your pool. Keep them shaded in the closed shipping bag while preparing to plant. Another way to keep them temporarily is to float them in your pond with wet newspaper over their stems and roots. Their leaves wither easily, especially the extremely thin day-bloomer leaves.

Prepare a hole for the root in the planting container, and place it in the soil carefully, packing the earth around it snugly but not too tightly. Cover the soil with gravel, making sure that the crown is not covered. Next, add pool water to the soil container, and then place the container in your pond.

Typical example of frost damage.

Hardy water lily—Gonnere, also known as Snowball.

Tropicals do best when they are first added to the pond if at least a few of their leaves float comfortably on the water's surface. Place the soil container at a depth shallow enough to permit at least two or three pads to float. Later, the container can be lowered in the water as the plant grows. Untangle the stems so the leaves can float easily, and make sure all leaves float right side up. It may take several days before they remain right side up. Meanwhile, adjust them whenever you visit your pond.

Deep Planting
Any of the containers I have suggested for pools can also be used in a natural pond. In deep water, where there is no danger of trampling by livestock and where the gardener has no intention of ever disturbing the plants, lilies can be set out in flimsy containers, or without containers at all. In fact, if they are used, the flimsiest of

containers are preferred, for they disintegrate quickly and allow the rootstock to spread and seek nourishment where they will.

Bushel and half bushel baskets serve the purpose nicely. Fill each one with heavy top soil, plant the root, and cover with a layer of stones to discourage interference from curious fish (being careful not to cover the growing point). Slip a rope through the basket handles, lower the basket into place, and then remove the rope.

There is also the old-fashioned method of planting lilies in deep water, which consists of tying a water lily root firmly to a brick, rowing out to the desired planting spot, and heaving root and brick overboard. Sometimes this puts extra stress on transplanted water lilies because they must endure several days with no pads able to reach the surface, so I do not favor this approach.

When planting in deep water, be sure to mark all the selected areas ahead of time with long poles. This enables you to hold to the planting pattern you wish. Once a plant has been lowered, even if the water is only three or four feet deep, it is practically impossible to find it until its leaves reach the surface, unless the planting place is so marked. If murky water prevents sunlight from reaching any of the pads, success is unlikely.

Planting In Shallow Water

Most professional growers, who can raise and lower the water level of their earth-bottom ponds at will, prefer to plant directly on the bottom, through about six inches of water. You can plant this way in any pond shallow enough for you to touch bottom with your hands. Sink the head of your shovel (at an angle) into the mud floor and pry up a wedge of soil. Then, place the lily root in position beneath the wedge, pull out the shovel, and press the wedge firmly over the root with

your foot. Be careful not to step on the crown, which should not be covered with soil.

For such free and natural planting as this, use only the Marliac type of water lilies if you want to keep control of them, for the Marliacs do not spread widely. Varieties of *odorata* and *tuberosa*, planted in an earth bottom pond, would soon take over the whole pond out to a depth of five or six feet of water if the soil is appropriate.

Tropicals can be planted freely anywhere in the frostbelt, without danger of taking over a pond. They will not survive repeated heavy frosts.

Winter Care, Repotting And Hunger Signs

Most American gardeners look upon tropical water lilies (actually frost tender perennials) as annuals. Frost kills them, so new ones must be installed each spring. A few gardeners overwinter their tropicals in greenhouses. In either case, tropical water lilies must be set

Hardy water lily—Sunrise, the largest of the hardy water lilies.

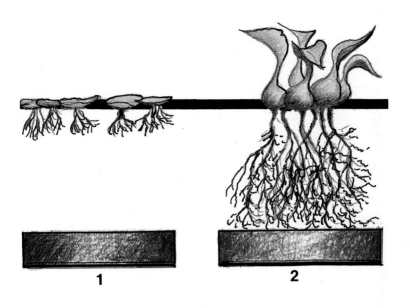

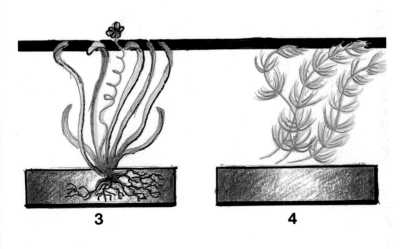

1) *Duckweed*, Spirodella. 2) *Water hyacinth*, Eichornia crassipes. 3) Vallisneria *sp.* 4) Ceratophyllum *sp.*

Planting the Pool

out anew in the outdoor pool each summer in frost-prone climates. They should be set out, of course, in a fresh supply of soil and fertilizer.

Hardy water lilies may be left in your pool from one year to the next provided the roots don't freeze, but you must remember to re-pot them occasionally. A hardy lily planted in 10 quarts of soil may have to be re-potted, even after one season, in areas where the growing season includes six or more frost-free months. If planted in something more spacious, say a container holding two cubic feet or more of soil, then a hardy lily will probably do well for two or three seasons—perhaps even longer—without requiring a change of soil.

It is good to lift the hardies every three or four years, whether they seem to need it or not, to prune them down a bit, and to trim a few of the growing points from the rootstocks.

Uproot a lily and replant it in a container of fresh soil and fertilizer in the beginning of its growing season. Lots of leaves, especially when some are held above the water's surface, and few, if any, blossoms are signs that your lily should be divided.

Occasionally, a lily will show signs of "hunger;" its leaves will be much smaller than they should be. They will be of a sickly yellow color, and its blooms (if any), will be small and few in number. Often the plant will show a general apathy and lack of healthy growth. Water lily fertilizer applied as directed, will usually correct such a situation.

The typically beautiful blossom of the water lily.

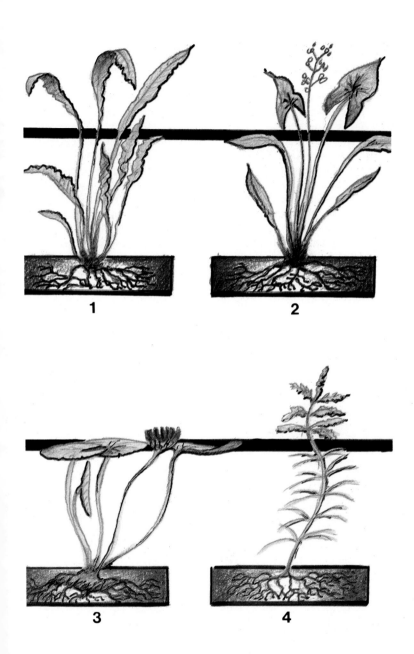

1) Cryptocoryne. 2) Sagittaria. 3) Nymphaea. 4) Proserpinaca.

Propagation, Culture, and Winter Care

The most widely used method of propagating hardy water lilies is rhizome division. Plants can be brought up from the bottom of the pool every spring for division in the parts of the country which have a long growing season. With shorter growing seasons, and/or with larger planting containers, you may bring them up less often for dividing. Remove them from the containers, divide the rhizomes, and replant using fresh supplies of soil and fertilizer.

Hardies can be divided successfully at any time in their normal growing season, from the time when the water temperature rises past 50° Fahrenheit until a month prior to frost. The disadvantage of disturbing the plants in their flowering season is that the disruption temporarily reduces the rate of blooming (about four weeks).

PROPAGATION OF HARDY WATER LILIES

Whether or not you want to start new plants, rhizome division is still helpful (every one, two, or three years) when using a 10-quart planting container. Rootstocks of some of the stronger growing forms, if left alone for four or five years, can become quite overgrown. At this stage many of them will stop blooming and will produce smaller and smaller leaves. Keep this in mind if the blooms and foliage of your plants begin to look sickly and listless after years of faithful, vigorous production. Division usually restores vigor.

By Root Division (Daughter Plants And Eyes)

Root division is a quick and simple operation. First, remove your plants from the soil and wash off the roots, so that you can see what you are doing. You will notice growing points (crowns), which look similar to what you might have purchased from an aquatic plant dealer, springing from the long, cylindrical *odorata* or *tuberosa* rhizomes and elongated Marliac rhizomes. With a sharp knife, divide each rootstock into four to six inch sections, making sure that each daughter section has a crown. Plant the four- to six-inch sections as you would the

A beautiful white water lily at its peak of perfection.

Illustration of potted hardy water lily showing rhizome at correct angle. Eye is producing new growth.

rootstocks purchased from a dealer.

The hybrids of *odorata* and *tuberosa* have rhizome eyes that can be easily broken off by hand, but you will need a knife to remove the eyes of the Marliac hybrids. Each eye should be planted in a six-inch pot of top soil, fertilized at the same ratio as given for adult plants and given no more than six inches of water over the soil. As the young plants increase in size, transfer them to larger soil containers and deeper water. The eyes produce blooming plants within their second or third growing season.

The Marliac pineapple-type rootstock is a thick, tight mass that seems more difficult to divide at first glance. Wash it off and then examine it carefully. You won't have much trouble recognizing the clean and tender growing points with bits of last season's stems clinging about them. With a sharp knife, cut the root clump into new plants, according to the growth of the eyes or the maturing daughter plants. Then set out the divisions as previously described for rhizome eyes or new water lilies.

When you divide roots you may have more left than you can give away. Although it seems a shame to dispose of potential beauty, it is far better to get rid of your extra stock than to overcrowd your pond.

By Seed + Hybridization

Some hardy water lilies can be propagated by seed, but it is a slow, painstaking process, with not much assurance to the amateur hybridizer of developing worthwhile plants. The Marliac hardies, as a group, are notoriously reluctant to set seed, and most that are produced are sterile. Despite the difficulties, however, working with seeds is extremely interesting, so, if you want to play the game for the game's sake and not for the prize alone, here is the procedure:

Make up your mind at the beginning whether you want to produce plants that will resemble parents, or if you want to develop a new hybrid. If you want to reproduce what you already have in the parents, you need only keep crossing parent plants, but be sure to protect them from stray pollen. You can help out with the pollination if you like, but most hardies that set seed at all are self-pollinating. If you want to try for a new hybrid, you must combine—or 'try' to combine—the colors and characteristics of two different species or varieties.

THE BEST TIME

To propagate next summer's water lilies by seed, begin with this summer's blooms. Select the pollen and the seed parents carefully, keeping in mind just what colors and characteristics you want to combine. Make sure that the seed parent you select is a fertile one. Many water lily varieties, especially among the hybrids, are sterile.

To determine for yourself if a water lily is self fertile, you pollinate it with its own pollen (instead of with pollen of another plant, as given below). If it produces no seed, it is either sterile or you did not correctly fertilize the plant. But if it produces seeds, then you know that it is fertile. Repeat this process with the other water lily you want to use in the cross.

If you have some water lilies you know are fertile, you can do more checking. To determine if the pollen of your water lily is fertile, use it on one or more varieties known to be seed fertile. To determine if it is seed fertile, use pollen from several varieties known to be pollen fertile. Sometimes good pollen from one variety but not from another will result in seed production.

Practically all varieties of *odorata*—particularly *caroliniana, gigantea, minor, rosea,* and *luciana—set enough seed to make any experiment worthwhile. This is also true of the varieties of alba, candida, flava, mexicana, pygmaea,* and *tetragona.* Another good bet is *tuberosa,* as are two of its cultivars, the Rosea and

Nuphar pumilum.

Richardsonii. You may also have fair luck with Gladstone.

SELECTING THE SEED PLANT

Now you must wait for nature to produce for you a set of circumstances favorable for hybridization. First, the bloom of the seed parent (female) plant must be freshly opened. You can watch a particular bud for a few days and get a pretty good idea of when it is going to break into bloom. The day or two before it would open by itself, cover it with a square-foot piece of cheesecloth to keep out insects that might introduce pollen from other plants. When the bloom opens naturally in the forenoon, trim off its anthers. A drop of clear sweet liquid, resting

Tropical night blooming lily, Mrs. George C. Hitchcock.

precisely in the middle of the stigma, plays an unknown function in propagation. Cover the bloom with cheesecloth to keep out insects.

SELECTING THE POLLEN PARENT AND MAKING THE CROSS

This flower, too, should be protected from stray pollen with a covering of cheesecloth. The pollen parent (male) flower that you select must be in its second or later day of blooming. This is absolutely necessary, because the pollen on the flower's anthers is not ripe and cannot be liberated from the anthers until the second day. With tweezers and a pair of manicure scissors, snip off several pollen-laden anthers. Transport them in a small jar to the waiting seed

In the wild, moths and butterflys play a larger role in the pollenization of water lilies than they do in commercial cultivation.

parent and uncover it. Then place the anthers carefully, pollen side down, upon the drop of liquid in the chosen seed parent flower. The cross has now been made, but this is only the first of several intricate steps in hybridization.

PROTECTING THE CROSS

Take the square of cheesecloth and cover the fertilized bloom, to protect it from further fertilization by insects—and wait. While you are

waiting, it might be a good idea to repeat the cross with other blooms.

DEVELOPMENT OF SEEDS

In about a week, if the cross has been unsuccessful, both the seed pod and the stem will begin to rot. If the hybridization took, the seed pod will begin to swell after a couple of weeks, dropping beneath the water as it enlarges. Tie a string around the stem of the seed parent, if you like, so that you can pull it up and look at it occasionally. Tie a cork or fishing bobble float on your string so that you can find it easily. The enlarging seed pod is the fruit of the water lily. When it is completely ripe, it will finally burst, scattering the seeds.

Seeds of the hardy water lilies are greenish-black or brown in color; some are like tiny apple seeds, others are somewhat larger and almost globular. Some varieties produce only six or seven seeds; others, particularly among the tropical species, produce hundreds of seeds.

If the seeds had not been caught by the cheesecloth that you fastened around the pod, they would have been kept afloat by their coating of colorless, mucilaginous matter. This is nature's way of allowing the seeds to float away from the mother plant, so that the offspring might establish themselves in new, less crowded places where they would have a better chance of survival. This buoyant seed coating disintegrates within a day and the seeds drop to the bottom.

Remove the seeds from the cheesecloth and put them in a jar of water. Then plant them as soon as possible after the coatings have dissolved, but keep the seeds in water until you do so. If you want to save them for another season, store them in a jar of distilled water in the refrigerator.

SOWING THE SEEDS

Fill a shallow pan with finely screened soil. Sow the seeds and cover them with a quarter inch or less of sand. Then gently lower the pan into water, to a depth of six inches below the water's surface.

Both the germinating seeds and the seedlings which develop from them will benefit from water that is kept at a temperature between 70° and 80°. Finally, the seedlings will appear, looking very much like tender new shoots of grass. Transplant them into two inch pots when they form their first floating leaves. If you have plenty of space, start them in larger containers.

CARE OF SEEDLINGS

From this point on the seedlings will require warm temperatures and full sun. As they grow, transplant them to larger soil containers. Fill the containers with the heavy top soil and add fertilizer as recommended for adult lilies.

After you plant it outside, wait as patiently as you can for your new hybrid to bloom. Who knows? Perhaps you will develop a hardy blue water lily. None currently exist. If you do, incidentally, please get in touch with me. I would trade you my hat and coat and practically anything else for such a gem!

Do not waste your time and effort trying to cross a hardy water lily with a tropical water lily, as they do not cross. Nor do day-blooming and night-blooming tropicals cross. These two categories of tropical water lilies are very different, botanically speaking.

By Runner

There is only one species of hardy water lily, to my knowledge, that reproduces by runner. This is *Nymphaea mexicana*, which sends out long, slender runners through the mud

The developer of this pond wisely sectioned off the area for the fountain from the lilies to provide the still water so beneficial to the culture of water lilies.

from its rootstock. The runners terminate in new plants, which take root, develop, and then send out runners of their own. If this species is not watched, it can make a spreading nuisance of itself.

FASCIATION

You have undoubtedly heard of people going to pieces under nervous strain, and there may have been times when you felt like it yourself. Once in a great while a water lily goes to pieces in a most complete and literal fashion. This happens when one is afflicted by a strange malformation called *fasciation*.

The sight is most alarming. If it occurs while you have been away for a weekend, you come back to plants that look as if a giant had taken a club and smashed the leaves into strange forms. One water lily plant may cover the whole end of a pool with these malformed leaves. Also, these plants do not have any normal blooms, large or small.

Nobody seems to know what causes fasciation. We know only that it happens to some water lilies when they get old, after they have bloomed normally and well for a number of years. And we know that some species and varieties are more prone to it than others. Ellisiana, Marliac

Carnea, Chromatella, Gloriosa, and Helvola are occasionally subject to this condition.

The main root of an affected plant is useless thereafter, so there is nothing to do but pull it out. It is difficult to examine the root closely, for it is covered with a tight and twisted mass of small leaves and stems. However, by removing some of the leaves you usually can find a few normal growing points. These can be cut off and planted as rootstocks. They then grow normally, and usually do not revert to fasciation, at least not for several years.

Don't worry about other water lilies in the pool. We do not know much about fasciation, but we do believe that it is not transmitted from one plant to another, and that most water gardeners never even observe it.

PROPAGATING TROPICAL WATER LILIES
By Seed – Hybridization

While water gardeners in frost-free areas know tropical water lilies as perennials, most water gardeners in the frostbelt treat tropical water lilies as annuals. They allow them to die off in winter and order new stock each spring. Even though the tropicals can be propagated in more ways than hardies, they do not propagate as easily as the hardies.

Propagation By Seed

As with the hardies, propagation of tropical water lilies by seed is a fascinating pursuit for those who want to take the trouble.

The procedure is the same as for the hardies, but infinitely more rewarding with tropical varieties. Many produce seed quite freely, and produce successfully from seed. However some tropical hybrids do not seed freely.

Some of the best seed-bearing day-blooming tropicals for seed production include Blue Capensis, Pink Capensis, and N. colorata.

Good night bloomers for seed production include Emily Grant Hutchings, Wood's White Knight, and Mrs. George C. Hitchcock.

To propagate tropical water lilies by seed, follow the directions for hardy water lilies up to the point of collecting the seeds. Seeds of tropical lilies are about the same size as poppy seeds. If you want to save them for the next season, store them dry. Allow the mucilaginous seed coating to disintegrate, and then air dry the seeds on newspaper. Keep them in a vial in a kitchen cabinet or on a pantry shelf.

Grow tropical water lilies from seed as you would hardy water lilies. Plant them outdoors, or in a greenhouse pool if the outdoor pool water is in danger of dropping below 70°.

Propagation By Tuber

Hybridizing and propagating tropicals by seed can be interesting, but there are surer, less troublesome ways, the simplest being by tuber. After a few frosts, dig up the tubers of the tropicals. If you don't have frosts or simply don't want to wait for them, you can force tropicals to form tubers by not

It is necessary to keep the crown, or growing tip, of tropical lilies free of soil.

feeding them. It helps if you use smaller than usual planting containers.

Tubers look like smooth black nuts or miniature sweet potatoes. Unique *N. colorata* produces several pea-sized tubers just outside the mother tuber. Wash the tubers thoroughly and remove all remnants of stems and roots. After cleaning and drying for several hours at room temperature, store them in a jar of cool, (40° to 50°), barely moist sand (several times the volume of the tubers being stored) for the winter. Only firm tubers survive storage. Cover the sandfilled jar tightly so that the tuber won't become dry. Some

of the tubers, even if they are kept moist, may rot. However, most of them should get through in good enough condition to plant when warm weather arrives.

Save only what healthy planting stock you need. Medium-sized, day-bloomer tubers are the easiest ones to work with. Examine the larger night-blooming tubers, the ones which disintegrate most readily. When this occurs you will notice that some contain tubers resembling small walnuts. These are new tubers. Remove them and store them at 40° to 50° in clean, damp sand, and most of them will survive. Some water gardeners report success in

Hardy lily roots wet below the ice line will safely survive the winter.

storing tubers in distilled water, while others report success in using sawdust instead of sand.

A month or two before you plan to plant the tubers outdoors, take them from the moist sand or other storage medium and plant them in soil in shallow water in a greenhouse or indoors with lots of sunlight. If kept at 70 to 80°, they will promptly sprout and produce plantlets in two to six weeks. Pinch the plantlets off when they have at least two floating leaves. Transfer the plantlets to pots, keep the pots submerged at an ever-increasing depth as the plants grow, and maintain them

this way until it is warm enough to move them outside to the pool. Tubers will continue to produce more plantlets for months before they become exhausted. Temperature is important. Another technique is to allow the daughter plants to remain attached to the mother tuber. At the end of the season the old tuber may be stored (if still firm) to use again next season.

Cooled to a temperature below 70°, sprouting tubers might go to sleep and either die or remain dormant for some time. With a greenhouse pool you can sprout tubers two to three months prior to the time for transplanting outdoors. By this time, your young plants may be budded.

PROPAGATING VIVIPAROUS DAY-BLOOMERS

Several day-blooming tropical water lilies have the mysterious faculty called **viviparity**, which is the ability to bear their young alive. A new baby water lily brought forth by viviparous reproduction is a sight that no flower lover will forget, and every water gardener should experience at least one viviparous water lily.

As the leaf of a viviparous water lily becomes mature, a discolored whitish bump forms at the umbilicus, the point where leaf and stem join. This bump breaks after a few days, and tiny, perfectly proportioned leaves begin to form and develop, sometimes growing to 1½ inches in diameter. Then, on some varieties, a perfectly formed miniature of the parent bloom unfolds, and the daughter plant produces its own offspring.

In the meantime, the tiny plant develops a root system, partially out of sight, on the underside of the leaf.

It is easy to nurse these miniatures to maturity. Simply pluck off a plant-bearing leaf and spread it flat on a pot of saturated earth, covered by one inch of water. Add water (or lower the pot) as the stems grow longer. Pin the leaf in place with nails. By the time the mother leaf has decomposed, the daughter plant has established itself as a healthy, growing tropical, ready for planting in the pool.

Often development at the leaf umbilicus contains several growing points and several root systems, the whole making up a multiple-headed plant. This can be easily divided. Nurse a multiple plant along as you would a single plant. When the individual growths become discernible—with a single growing crown to each—remove the plants from the pot and divide them gingerly with your fingers. An unaltered multiple plant produces foliage and blooms, but not as big as those of a plant divided off and allowed to grow alone.

Those tropical varieties which are viviparous are, as a group, somewhat smaller in growth than the others, on average. However, they have been crossed with a number of the larger varieties so that now we have several viviparous hybrids of tremendous size.

Among the water lilies, only day-blooming tropicals are viviparous (except for Colonel A. J. Welch, a yellow hardy which forms daughter plants directly from the flower pod). Dauben, Mrs. Martin E. Randig and Panama Pacific are especially viviparous. Charles Thomas, Margaret Mary and Pink Platter are also viviparous.

Viviparity varies with the location. It shows up at its best in the tropics. In cooler climates its vigor is reduced.

WINTER CARE OF POND

There are several ways of carrying hardies through the winter.

Most gardeners simply remove whatever stones and bricks they have placed underneath the planting containers so as to let the containers rest on the pool floor. This will put them well below the ice line in most parts of the world, where they can safely survive the winter. Roots of the hardies are not harmed unless actually frozen solid in ice.

If the ice depth goes dangerously low in your country, you could play it safe by covering the pool with boards. Then cover the boards with leaves, evergreen boughs, straw, or any other convenient insulation. Some prefer to cover their pools with canvas or polyethylene that is placed over beams. If you cover yours, be sure not to seal it. Allow for some air passage so that carbon dioxide and other gases may escape and be replaced with oxygen, which your fish will require. Guard against anyone accidentally stumbling into the covered pool.

Other gardeners prefer to use a submersible pump that will discharge water vertically an inch or two below the surface. The warmer bottom water makes an interesting sight while keeping an ice-free area. If you use this method, be sure to check your pool occasionally. Should there be a power outage long enough to freeze water in the discharge pipe, ice blocking the pipe would render this technique useless.

Another method of providing extra winter safety is the use of a pool de-icer.

You can also overwinter the rootstock of hardies indoors.

Take them inside in their planting containers but trim off leaves and stems. Store them in a cool area (40° to 45°), but do not allow them to freeze. Place moist material over them, and cover them with plastic trash bags so that they will stay moist, and be sure to check them several times through the winter. Also beware of rodents that may want to eat them.

I know gardeners who winter hardy water lilies in all these ways, and each thinks his or her way is best. Certainly where you live can influence which method that you prefer.

WINTERING TROPICAL WATER LILIES

In areas which do not have killing frosts, tropical water lilies can be left outdoors in your pool the year around, and cultivated much the same as for hardies. Tropicals are frost tender perennials that bloom until their foliage is killed by repeated frost. Being heavy feeders, they should be given a new supply of soil each spring if they are planted in containers. On their own in a natural mud bottom pond, they probably will not need annual replanting.

In the frostbelt, however, tubers of tropicals must be taken inside if they are to be kept alive. Their winter storage method (in cool clean, damp sand) was covered previously.

Some of those rare enthusiasts who maintain indoor pools with greenhouse-like conditions have had good luck with the winter culture of

Dauben, Margaret Mary, and other tropicals which bloom with comparatively little direct sunlight. Sunny window positions tend to provide too little direct sunlight. The minimum water temperature should be no lower than 65°, but I prefer to recommend 70° as the minimum.

DAY-TO-DAY CARE

The day-to-day culture of water lilies amounts to casual grooming from time to time. Keep an eye on your more expansive lilies and accessory aquatics. If they produce more foliage than you want, cut and discard the excess leaves. If you do so, cut, or pinch off down near the rootstock, leaving no stems to decompose and foul the pond water. Remove the stems of expired blooms in the same way and for the same reason. Also, cutting off old blossoms will encourage additional blooming.

Water gardening can be quite easy after planting your pool. Be patient while the pool inhabitants and water adjust to one another. This process requires six to eight weeks. Refrain from making the mistake of changing the water when it turns green during the first few weeks. Doing so only means beginning the six to eight week adjusting period again.

Unlike for land plants, you need not worry about over or under watering the aquatics. Naturally, you will need to replace evaporated water that is not replaced naturally by rain. And best of all, there's no hoeing or weeding. Not even dandelions will grow in your garden pool!

Marginal plants accent the decor of your pond, creating a totally unified and harmonious environment.

This is a chapter my water gardening friends have, to a large extent, helped me write, for it consists principally of my answers to the questions they most frequently ask. This summary must necessarily be generalized. I enjoy sharing information with water gardening enthusiasts.

BEST KINDS TO CUT

One or two water lilies floating in a large glass, silver, or ceramic bowl, with a lily pad for background, make an effective arrangement. And, generally speaking, any water lily that pleases you can be cut for a table centerpiece or other decoration. Those hardies which seem to hold up best indoors as cut flowers include Hollandia, Virginalis, Marliac Carnea, Comanche, Chromatella, James Brydon, and Escarboucle. Other good hardies for cutting include Gladstone, Gonnere, Attraction, and Pink Opal.

Among the best tropicals for cutting are the day-blooming Robert Strawn, Aviator Pring, Blue Beauty, Mrs. Martin E. Randig, Pamela, Mrs. C. W. Ward, and White Delight; and the night-blooming Wood's White Knight, Red Flare, and Emily Grant Hutchings.

Choosing Cut Flowers

Most water lilies, growing normally in a pool, open their blooms for three or four consecutive days or nights. But water lilies sometimes extend their normal performance by a

Gladstone, a hardy water lily.

Above: *Hollandia.* **Below:** *Masaniello.*

Pink Opal.

day when cut and taken into the house.

Both hardies and tropicals make good cut flowers. To get the best out of them, select first day blooms for cutting. If you have a small pool, this will not be much of a trick. If you have a large pool, with several dozen water lilies blooming at once, you will have to learn to recognize a newly borne flower. Look for a blossom in which stamens are not yet curled. Look for plump, round anthers which have not yet begun to shed pollen, and for a stigma with the tiny basin still holding a droplet of nectar.

First day blooms open an hour later and close an hour earlier than older flowers. Both the opening of a flower and its closing take about an hour.

Usually the hardies and day-blooming tropicals, after being cut, will follow their normal habits and open their blossoms the same as if they were still in the pool. The night-blooming tropicals, when cut, usually follow their normal routine and stay open from about dusk until well into the following morning, but not always. Sometimes a combination of factors—temperature, humidity, light—will cause blooms to fold up into buds at odd times or to remain open unexpectedly.

How To Keep Blooms Open
There are two sure ways of keeping blooms open. You can

place the stems in a vase of ice water, and store them in the refrigerator until it is time to use them as decorations. They will then remain open for a few hours after being removed from the refrigerator. Or you can let the blooms unfold to their fullest before cutting them, and then put a drop of melted paraffin or wax from a lighted candle at the point where petals and sepals join the base. Hardening, the paraffin or wax forms an unseen but sturdy cast which holds blooms open.

A word of caution: water lilies set out in this way as decoration bear up well under summer heat and even a bit of handling, but a sustained draft of air will kill them. So don't set them directly in front of an air conditioner or an open window. Also, cut the stems of the hardies short enough so that no more than an inch or so of stem is exposed above the water. Water lilies are attractive when floating in a bowl. Lotus blossoms are also sensitive to a draft of air, but their stems may be exposed to several inches of air.

LIST OF BESTS

Hardly a day goes by that I do not answer at least one letter from a water gardener who wants a water lily with some specific and outstanding characteristic—the tallest, the widest, the reddest, the most fragrant, and so on. Here are some recommendations:

Attraction.

Lists of Bests

Earliest
Gladstone, Virginalis, *N. odorata gigantea*, Chromatella, Comanche Pink Sensation, Sumptuosa, and Rose Arey Hybrid can be depended upon, just about anywhere, to be among the first to bloom each season.

Largest Flowers
Virginia, Escarboucle, Attraction, and Sunrise among the hardies; White Delight, Aviator Pring, Pink Platter among the day-blooming tropicals; Red Flare, Maroon Beauty, and Emily Grant Hutchings among night-blooming tropicals.

Most Prolific Bloomers
Fabiola, James Brydon, Gloriosa, Chromatella, Pink Sensation, and Marliac Carnea for the hardies; the tropical day-blooming Dauben, Blue Beauty, Director Moore; and the night-blooming tropical Wood's White Knight, Emily Grant Hutchings and Red Flare are free-blooming with a fine, long succession of flowers.

Most Fragrant
The most fragrant hardies are *N. odorata gigantea*, Mrs. C. W. Thomas, and Rose Arey. All day-blooming tropicals are fragrant, most of them very fragrant.

Director George T. Moore, tropical day bloomer.

Above: *Emily Grant Hutchings.*
Below: *Rose Arey Hybrid.*

103

Pink Platter.

With Double Blossoms

The double-flowered water lilies
with most distinctive forms, in
my opinion, include among the
hardies James Brydon and
Gonnere, and among the day-
blooming tropicals, those of
White Delight and Pink Platter.

For Deep Pools

Water lilies that flourish in
deeper than ordinary pools
include James Brydon,
Escarboucle, Attraction, Radiant
Red, Virginia, Queen of Whites,
odorata gigantea, Gladstone,
and Marliac Carnea, all hardies.
For years I have grown Blue

Beauty in five feet of water. It
faithfully produces an abundance
of flowers.

For Shallow Pools

Hardies which do well in shallow
pools, say a foot or even less of
water, include James Brydon,
Gloriosa, Helvola, Jo Ann Pring,
Marliac Carnea, Fabiola and
Chromatella.

Practically all day- and night-
blooming tropicals do well in
shallow water. Dauben tolerates
four inches of water over the
soil.

For Tubs and Miniature Pools

The shallow-water hardies listed
above are all fine for tub culture

Above: *Blue Beauty.* **Below:** *Gladstone.*

and very small pools.
Recommended tropicals include day-bloomers Dauben, Colorata, Charles Thomas, Marian Strawn, and Panama Pacific.

Best Lake Lilies

For lake and pond planting of the hardy water lilies use the Marliac varieties. These varieties tend to stay put in clumps which do not spread widely. Suggested clump type hardies for the lake or pond

Practically all tropical water lilies are good for pond planting, provided the soil is suitable and the water depth is not much more than four feet. Their major drawback in climates with repeated frosts is that they must be replanted each year.

For Indoor Winter Culture

I have never seen an indoor pool that would satisfactorily grow

James Brydon.

are Escarboucle, Attraction, Hollandia, Marliac Carnea, Gladstone, James Brydon, and Virginia.

For those who want water lilies to spread, *N. odorata* and *N. tuberosa* varieties are recommended. I like *odorata gigantea*, Helen Fowler, Mrs. C. W. Thomas and Charlene Strawn.

water lilies (except those few that imitate a greenhouse environment). You can grow them readily in a greenhouse pool in winter.

In Less Than Full Sun

Direct sunlight is a necessary stimulant for flower production, and the more of it that a water lily receives, the more profuse

Marliac albida, *also called Marliac White.*

Above: *General Pershing, tropical day bloomer.*

Below: *N. colorata, tropical day bloomer.*

will be the blooming. However, there are a few varieties which are so free-blooming that even a few hours of sun will produce a satisfactory number of blossoms.

These hardy water lilies produce blooms with as little as three to four hours of direct sun: Virginia, Marliac Carnea, Masaniello, Charlene Strawn, Chromatella, Helvola, Attraction, Gloriosa, James Brydon, Sirius and Comanche.

The following tropical day-bloomers bloom with as little as three to four hours of direct sun: Dauben, Charles Thomas, *N. colorata,* Robert Strawn, Mrs. Martin E. Randig, Panama Pacific, Director Moore, St. *Daubeniana.*

Louis, General Pershing, and Albert Greenberg.

Viviparous
Strongly viviparous: Dauben, Charles Thomas, Panama Pacific, Mrs. Martin E. Randig.

Best By Color
New water gardeners frequently ask me to recommend the best water lily in a certain color. To avoid argument, I want to stress that I give here my personal preferences. Describing and ranking beautiful flowers is like describing and ranking beautiful paintings—people can't agree on the same ranking.

RED. The hardy Escarboucle and James Brydon; the tropical

Red Flare.

night-blooming Red Flare and H. C. Haarstick.

YELLOW. Chromatella, Charlene Strawn, and Sunrise among hardies, and these tropicals—the day-blooming Aviator Pring and Yellow Dazzler.

WHITE. The hardy Virginia and Virginalis; the tropical day-blooming White Delight, and the night-blooming Wood's White Knight.

PINK. The hardy Fabiola and Pink Sensation; the tropical day-blooming General Pershing.

CHANGEABLES. The hardy Comanche.

BLUE. The day-blooming Blue Beauty, Director George T. Moore.

There is no blue hardy water lily, nor is there a blue night-blooming tropical.

Best Six

Probably the most thumbed page of one water lily firm's catalog every year, judging by the orders received, is that page devoted to a selection of six good water lilies with which new gardeners can begin. I assist in the selection process. We select with an eye to variety of color, flower form, availability and blooming habit. And, of course, I include only those water lilies which I know grow readily for amateurs.

I confine my selections to the hardies, because I find that most new gardeners are mainly

Above: *Yellow Dazzler.* **Below:** *Aviator Pring.*

Persian Lilac.

interested in first establishing
hardy, perennial growers. Most
water gardeners grow the
tropicals only as annuals,
selecting a few of them each
year, usually preferring to try
different forms and colors with
each new selection. These are
the six hardies I have selected:
Hollandia, Virginia, Virginalis,
Charlene Strawn, James Brydon,
and Fabiola.

112

The care and cultivation of your pond is a pleasant, healthful task which may be shared by the whole family. Children are fascinated by ponds. The complete ecological environment existing in your pond will create a wonderful vehicle to explain some of the mysteries of life to curious young minds.

1) Pygmaea Helvola.
2) *Aurora.*
3) *Marliac Red.*
4) *Hermine.*

Margaret Randig.

First Cousins of the Water Lilies

Lotus. A close-up of an improved type of Nelumbo nucifera, *showing the seed pod.*

Other genera of the water lily family *Nymphaeaceae* might be considered as first cousins of water lilies. Like cousins, these various flowering plants bear the same family name and have a certain family resemblance. Like cousins, they spring from a common ancestor. They are grouped under one family name because they have developed along the same lines and have in common various structural characteristics and habits. The family also has its plainer genera, including water shields, and *Cabomba*. The most important similarity is that of flower structure—which the botanist uses as the key in assigning a plant to a particular family.

GENUS *VICTORIA*— GRANDEST OF ALL

I include this magnificent genus of aquatic plants (consisting of only two species) with academic rather than practical intent, since few non-professionals have time, space, or patience to cultivate it. Gardeners for estates and public parks, however, find it worthwhile for it is the most spectacular of all the aquatics. And if you live near a park or garden in which a *Victoria amazonica* (Amazon water lily) is growing, you will find the sight well worth the effort of a Saturday or Sunday excursion. Certainly hundreds of people drive miles on late summer weekends to see the *Victoria* wherever they are on public display.

The foliage of this plant is striking, for the leaves often measure six feet or more across, and have edges that turn up to form a straight-sided rim. Leaves are rich green above and appear to be quilted in a geometric pattern. Underneath they are heavily marked with thick, barbed veins radiating from the center. The compartments formed by the network of veins are filled with a gas that is trapped by the leaf cells. It is this gas, trapped in the leaf, that makes it so buoyant.

The flower is also enormous, up to 16 inches across, but more often 8 to 12 inches in diameter. It exudes a heady fragrance like crushed pineapple. This plant is night blooming, and it opens for two consecutive evenings, creamy-white at first, passing on

Charles Thomas Lotus.

the second night to light pink, then deeper pink, and finally to rose-red.

The seed pod, which is as large as half a grapefruit and is covered with sharp spines, contains a cluster of hard, shiny, light brown seeds.

Species and Varieties

Victoria amazonica is, of course, the most widely known species of the genus, with flower and leaf of the classic form just discussed. It has a purplish-red underside. Spines are on its sepals. A native of tropical South America, *V. amazonica* does poorly outdoors in temperate zones. It was formerly known as *V. regia*.

V. cruziana—is a somewhat hardier South American form from Paraguay. It requires a little less heat than *V. amazonica*. Flowers are similar but appear earlier and without spines on sepals. The foliage is green on top and violet to green underneath. It produces the largest lip of any *Victoria*.

V. cruziana x. amazonica (Longwood) was developed by Patrick Nutt of Longwood Gardens, Kennett Square, Pennsylvania. It is a favorite in temperate climates because it tolerates coolness better than do other *Victoria*, and its red color, on the outside of the pad rims, commands extra attention. The sepals have spines to their tips. Longwood produces more and larger blossoms than either of its parents.

SEEDS TO POOL

Since it is a frost-tender perennial, the *Victoria* has to be treated as an annual in climates having frost, and it must be given more of practically everything—sun, space, heat, time, patience, and care—than any other aquatic. Seeds are gathered in fall and stored in bottles of water to keep them from drying out. The hard shells are penetrated by filing or cutting, and are then planted in the winter, in shallow pans of fine, unfertilized soil with three to four inches of water. At this stage, they are kept at 70° to 80° for *V. cruziana* and 85° to 90° for *V. amazonica (regia)* and exposed to full sunlight.

The more active seeds begin to germinate in one to three weeks. As soon as seedlings form their second tiny submerged leaves, they are moved to submerged three-inch

A true lotus, Nelumbium *sp. Notice the characteristic seed capsules at the left.*

pots filled with screened, heavy garden top soil. A fraction of a water lily fertilizer tab is then added. As the plants grow, they are moved to larger and larger pots, finally reaching a 10-inch size. They are at this point ready to be set outdoors in the pool, but not before the low daily water temperature is 75°.

Victoria should have a pool at least 10 feet (preferably larger)

Tulip lotus.

across and 18 inches deep in the center. Planting containers should have minimum dimensions of 18 inches across and nine inches deep (bigger is better), and must be filled with the same mixture of heavy loam and fertilizer that is required by the hardy and tropical water lilies. *Victoria* are set into the soil much as tropicals are buried up to, but not over, their growing points. Planted outdoors in full sun as soon as the season has become consistently warm, *Victoria* produce new foliage quickly, but the blooms usually do not develop until stimulated by several weeks of over 80°F weather in the full summer.

Only three forms are in cultivation, and these are comparatively rarely grown.

GENUS *NELUMBO*

Lotus are one of the oldest flowering plants in the world, and have been admired—even revered—through the ages for their awe-inspiring beauty. Lotus have been featured in some of the earliest known crude drawings, and the Egyptians, it is said, made them the parent of ornamentation. Certainly lotus were a basic motif in early Assyrian and Persian art.

A native of India, lotus were sacred to the ancient Hindus, the bloom representing their country, and the leaves representing the surrounding countries and cultures. To the Buddhists, they symbolized the most exalted representation of man—his head held high, pure and undefiled in the sun, his feet

119

rooted in the world of experience.

In other times, to other peoples, the magnificent blooms of the lotus, fed by roots buried in the mud, have symbolized a king with a common touch, beauty coming from filth and squalor, hope arising from chaos. In very early civilizations, the lotus flower was the emblem of female beauty and fertility—a symbol of life itself. Most lotus varieties (whites, pinks, and reds) are Asian. There is one American species, the *Nelumbo lutea.*

I have heard people describe lotus as big water lilies. They are not water lilies. But, as a group, they are big plants—bigger than water lilies. Blooms, foliage, and rootstock are formed differently from water lilies.

How Lotus Grow

Initially lotus produce pads that float on the water. The leaves, usually bluish-green, are round, often two feet across, gently frilled at the edge, without sinus, and without the customary water lily notch at the junction of stem and leaf. They are produced throughout the growing season. Once these appear, they are soon joined by aerial leaves. They are shaped like shallow bowls and are without the water lily notch. The leaves hold rain water for hours after a shower. Stems range in length from 1½ feet on miniatures to 8 feet on full size lotus. A five-foot stem is quite customary. An aerial leaf

with its stem looks rather like a parasol, and sometimes so used.

Leaf surfaces are covered with thin layers of wax, which causes drops of dew and rain to sparkle in the sun and roll around on the leaves like quicksilver—a beautiful sight. In some forms, leaves are covered with a fine, floury nap, which is also waterproof, and dew and rain water spell magic on these plants, too.

The huge and showy blooms, like tremendous, full blown roses, are frequently 10 to 12 inches across, and are borne high above the water on long, stout stems. Lotus blooms open over a period of three days, at first partially, then more fully on the second day, and finally, on the third, they unfold completely. After that, petals begin to drop away.

When they grow near the shore close to trees and other seed-bearing plants, lotus leaves catch not only rain water but also airborne seeds. Often these seeds sprout, and the lotus leaves become miniature roof gardens. I have seen such leaves bearing up to 30 two- and three-inch seedlings.

Most lotus have blooms that are fragrant, some quite powerfully so. Scents are distinctive and comparable to no other flower. The fragrance of the lotus is usually described as mysterious or oriental. It seems somewhat like anise.

A most interesting feature is the big funnel-shaped seed pod.

At first this is yellow and not so hard. When the petals fall, it turns green and swells. Then it dries and becomes brown, rather hard and woody. It has a form much prized for winter bouquets and wreaths, to which lotus pods give attractive variation.

Nymphaea lotus dentata *plantlet, a tropical night blooming water lily being started in an aquarium.*

REPRODUCTION

When you order a lotus from a dealer, be sure to do so early in the season, because tubers are available for only six or eight weeks before they turn into runners (which do not transplant very well).

When you order early, you should receive a tuber approximately 8 to 18 inches long. These tubers will have an elongated, cylindrical, brittle body, sometimes as thick as a broom handle, a single (or double) growing point, and two or more joints. If planted during the first two weeks of availability, the properly planted lotus tuber produces profuse foliage, and usually blooms the first year.

A lotus reproduces most quickly through its long, slender rootstock, which forms a joint every 5 to 18 inches, with a tapered growing point at the end. Leaves sprout and grow from each joint formed by the running growing point. Under ideal conditions and when planted in an earth bottom pond, a section of rootstock may develop a 20-foot runner in a single season.

Usually, a lotus sends out a single fairly straight chain-like runner—composed of one elongated section that grows from the tip of another. The direction the runner takes is influenced by different factors. It will seek rich, watery earth in which to send up new plants, and it will grow around areas of hard, rocky earth. A growing point may show itself briefly above the ground or water

surface, then submerge again as the rootstock extends itself.

Thus a lotus planted in one spot of an earth-bottom pond may send its roots beneath a sidewalk and crop up in some totally unexpected place. In view of this vigorous spreading habit, coupled with a stubborn tendency to remain wherever it becomes established, you can plan on it taking over a vast area of a pond. Many water gardeners beautifully decorate great sections of their estates, creating a tropical appearance, by letting lotus do just that.

Though sometimes slow to start, a lotus grows quickly and strongly when it becomes established. The rootstock is tender, and flees from frost. As the weather turns colder, it sends its root deeper and deeper into the mud, sometimes to a depth of two feet. By the time frost kills off the foliage, the plant will have established a goodly length of rootstock safely below the frost line. As the weather becomes warmer, the growing root heads for the surface again.

A lotus can also be propagated by its seeds, though it is a hit-or-miss proposition. Remove the brown seeds—each resembles the meaty part of an acorn—from their dried pods in autumn. Store them in a cool dry place. Score the tough seed shells with a file, and in late winter plant them an inch deep in a six inch pot of earth. Keep the pot submerged in a sunny location until warm weather is established, then transfer each

Nymphaea alba.

sprouting seedling to a planting box in the outdoor pool.

CULTIVATION

A lotus is typically planted in a plastic tub 16 to 20 inches in diameter and 9 to 10 inches deep.

Use the same kind of soil and fertilizer prescribed for hardy water lilies.

To plant, scoop out a depression in a receptacle filled with soil to within four inches of the rim. Place the root in the depression and cover with an inch or so of earth, letting half an inch of the growing tip or tips stick out. *This is the secret of success; growing tip or tips must absolutely stick out of the soil.*

Lay a flat rock on the covered root (it may float if you don't), being careful not to touch the fragile growing point. This waxen, brittle point is exceedingly tender, and can be killed by careless handling. Add fertilizer as you would for water lilies. Cover the soil with gravel, again avoiding the growing point. Next, gently add water from your pool to the newly planted soil. When the water replaces all of the air in the soil, it is ready to be submerged into your pool.

Set the planting container into the pool in such a position that the tip of the lotus is covered by five inches of water. As the stems grow longer, move the soil container to deeper water. Established plants enjoy 6 to 12 inches of water, but I have seen them blooming in water three to four feet deep.

If the container is watertight, it may be placed on a sunny porch or terrace, or out on the lawn. In this case, the soil would be filled to allow for at least five inches of water over the root. Keep the receptacle filled to the brim with water. A couple of small goldfish swimming around at the base of the growing lotus adds interest, and the fish eat mosquito larvae that may appear in the water.

You may plant the lotus rootstock in a natural pond at a depth of five or six inches. Point the root in the direction in which spreading is desired. Vigorous though it is, the lotus is sometimes slow to get established. Newly planted lotus, in some cases, produce a wealth of foliage and blooms the first season. In other cases, they may produce only some foliage the first summer. Nearly all produce heavily by the second year.

The quickest, most abundant growers are Lutea, Speciosum, Roseum Plenum, and Mrs. Perry D. Slocum.

WINTER CARE

Planted in a natural pond and given freedom, a lotus takes care of itself. Growing in a receptacle, either in or out of the pool, it also takes care of itself, provided water does not freeze down to the growing tip of the root. It is killed if ice touches this point. If there is such danger, take the plant (in its soil container) indoors when the foliage dies

Lotus tubers need to be planted in an 8-gallon tub or larger. The depth of the tub can be adjusted with brick or stone to achieve the optimal water level.

125

down in fall. Keep the soil moist and the plant cool, that is, about 40°, through the winter. Be sure rodents don't have access to it, for they love to eat the roots.

Every couple of years, very carefully remove the roots from the planting container. This is best accomplished early in the spring, when you discover the first leaf. Fill the container with a fresh supply of soil and fertilizer, and plant one healthy new section of rootstock, broken from the parent plant. You will have a number of root sections left over to increase your own plantings, if you wish, or to share with friends. Allow a growing tip

plus two or more joints to each section of rootstock broken or cut off for planting elsewhere. In dividing a section of rootstock, divide midway between joints.

AVAILABLE LOTUS VARIETIES
Nearly 100 forms of lotus are known, but only a comparatively few are distributed commercially. Most dealers carry only three or four varieties of lotus, and it is a rare find to discover a dealer offering more than a dozen. **Alba Grandiflora** has very fragrant, large, rounded white petals. **Charles Thomas**, U.S. Plant Patent 5794. Perry Slocum developed a winner with this carmine/rose lotus which holds the blossom well above the foliage. Second day blossoms show a touch of lavender. **Empress** has white petals fringed with crimson. Very striking. The native North American **Lutea** produces light yellow flowers. The rose-colored **Momo Botan** is excellent for smaller ponds or whiskey barrels. Leaves average 12 to 18 inches in diameter. **Miniature Momo Botan** has small, 4- to 12-inch leaves. Superb choice for smaller containers—16-inch diameter and up. Very large rose double flowers. **Mrs. Perry D. Slocum** has outstanding, large blossoms that change color from deep pink to creamy yellow. **Red**

The statue/fountain arrangement in this pool does not produce enough turbulence to disturb these water lilies. Note the attractive mottled leaves of some of the lilies.

Lotus is a deep rose red with large-petaled flowers. **Roseum Plenum** has very large, double, rosy pink flowers. **Shiroman's** large, double blossoms are cream-colored with a few petals of a light green tint. As it ages, the blossom becomes pure white. Good cut flower.

Speciosum is very fragrant with wide-petaled, light pink flowers.

The **Tulip Lotus**, which grows to 18 inches high, is well-suited to culture in small containers. It produces creamy white tulip-shaped flowers.

GENUS *NUPHAR*

Nuphar, or spatterdock, is also known as Cow Lily and Yellow Pond Lily. In form and habit, it seems similar to, yet is distinctly different from, the hardy water lily.

Its thick leaves are like those of the hardies except that they tend toward heart shapes, and sometimes float. Often they are held inches above the water. At the end of a thick stem, the plant supports a two to three inch bloom with usually six golden-yellow, concave sepals. The bloom is cup-shaped, and almost spherical. Most casual observers mistake the sepals for petals. Actually, it has numerous petals, but they are so insignificant that they appear to be a cluster of short stamens. *Nuphar* thrive in either warm, still pools or in cool, running streams, and can be found growing in the wild across mainland United States, including Alaska. They are very hardy, and survive in places where hardy and tropical water

Nymphoides peltata.

lilies cannot grow.

It is widely claimed that *Nuphar* thrive without sun, but I have yet to have the claim proven. I know it can produce a great deal of foliage in deep shade, but I have never seen a fully shaded *nuphar* produce blooms. It is rarely cultivated in a garden pool, because its blossoms are smaller than those of most water lilies and its foliage is larger than that of most hardies. Also, its flower opens later than do water lily blossoms, while closing earlier. Moreover, *Nuphar* are shy bloomers compared to water lilies. But a cluster of *Nuphar* in a natural pond—where they are only a small, incidental part of the show—adds interest and some color to the view.

Red Lotus—Capiscium.

Plant and propagate *Nuphar* the same as you would hardy water lilies. There are species which grow wild practically all over the world. These are the more common North American forms.

Species and Varieties

Nuphar advenum—One of the most common species. Leaves about one foot wide, round to oblong, with a wide notch at the point where stem joins leaf. Blooms, two to three inches in diameter, have bright yellow sepals touched with green or purple, with deep yellow or pale red stigma. Both blooms and foliage held above the water.

N. kalmianum—A much smaller species, with floating leaves no larger than saucers and a pale yellow bloom one inch or less in diameter. Spreads swiftly in the shallow water along the margin of a pond or river.

N. macrophyllum—Strong growing warm climate species with bloom similar to that of *N. kalmianum*. Foliage, however, is large and ovate. One of the few members of the water lily family which will grow in running water.

N. minimum—Also known as Dwarf Pond Lily. A very free flowering species with tiny, pale yellow blooms and miniature floating leaves.

N. orbiculatum—A large and robust warm climate species with round, bright green leaves somewhat fluted at the edges.

Views of the giant Victoria water lily in the Rio das Mortes region of Brazil. A jacana, or lily trotter, a tropical marsh bird, strolls across the surface of a Victoria lily pad. The mature leaves of this aquatic pad are reportedly large enough to support the weight of a grown man.

This lovely pool is constantly supplied with oxygenated water from the gently sloping waterfall.

Ted Uber.

Yellowish blooms about two inches wide. Stems and undersides of leaves covered with white down.

N. polysepalum—One of the largest of the North American species. Leaves are elongated, and the yellow bloom is four to five inches wide. Both blooms and leaves stand out of the water along the shore, float in deeper water.

N. rubrodiscum—Also called Red Disk Pond Lily. The elongated leaves range from 3 to 10 inches in length, float in deep water, stand erect in shallow. Yellow blooms, less than 2 inches in diameter, with conspicuous red centers.

EURYALE FEROX

Euryale ferox falls into a little known genus of the water lily family. Once, before *Victorias* were discovered, it was the giant of the family.

It is indigenous to China, Japan, and India. Its flat, floating leaves reach four to five feet in diameter. Its purple blooms are smaller than those of most water lilies, and for this reason it has never become popular with water gardeners.

For plant size, however, it commands a certain respect. It is an annual that grows well in outdoor ponds, and re-seeds itself from year to year.

The banana plant is a desirable novelty in aquariums. It will flower when placed outdoors in ponds. It blooms only in direct sunlight.

Nuphar luteum.

Ornamental Fish and Scavengers

Even though these koi are quite large, they live together in harmony with water lilies.

Your pool will have added interest when it is stocked with ornamental fish. Fish provide colorful, animated movement to any water garden. They can become beloved pets, and often are named. It is soothing to sit and watch your fish swim lazily about. And what a thrill it is when your fish know you well enough to eat out of your hand. Some fish even enjoy being stroked.

Fish are an important part of the balanced ecological system that you should establish in your pool. A rule of thumb for typical garden pools is to allow three gallons of water per inch of fish. You will find some water gardeners who successfully allow only a gallon of water per

Koi are available in millions of color patterns and color combinations. Like snowflakes, no two are exactly alike.

inch of fish, but by stocking on the light side, your fish will grow more and they will be much more likely to reproduce. This is a delight for all members of the family.

A very important reason to

have at least a few fish in your pond is that they will prevent your pond from becoming a mosquito factory. Goldfish, koi, and golden orfes all love to eat mosquito larvae.

In the spring you can observe nature at its best when your fish begin to spawn. The excitement increases as the babies first appear and then begin to grow. These ideal pets are responsive, yet undemanding. No housebreaking, fencing, or

A formal, Japanese-style pool. The koi in this pool need auxillary feeding, as they are hearty eaters and would not be able to glean adequate sustenance from the natural food sources available.

Ducks would likely feast on small fish in your pond, but judging from the size of the fish in this pond, this duck will have to go elsewhere for dinner.

walking is required. You won't even have to worry about hiring a fish sitter if you go out of town. Your fish can live for weeks on submerged plants and the volunteer moss-like algae naturally growing on the sides of pools.

Purchase your fish from a reliable source, and select fish which have been bred and raised outdoors. They will be much sturdier and better suited for your water garden, since they will be accustomed to the elements, especially changes in water temperature. Look for fish that are alert, with erect dorsal (top) fins and clear eyes. Avoid fish which are sluggish, and laying at the bottom of the tank, or that have closed fins.

GOLDFISH (*Carassius auratus*)
There are two basic types of goldfish—scaled and scaleless. The scaled goldfish, Comet, Japanese Fantail, Black Chinese Moor, and others, are silvery olive-gray when hatched. The back becomes a velvety black while the familiar gold (sometimes with pearly white) emerges on the sides. Eventually, the black top yields to the gold (or pearly white) as the fish assume their characteristic bright metallic coloration. Moors gradually turn from silvery olive-gray to velvety black. With advanced age Moors sometimes develop gold scales. However, a small percentage of goldfish never color.

The scaleless fish, Shubunkins and Calico Fantails, actually have transparent scales which look like delicate skin. Sometimes a few regular metallic-like scales provide a special accent. And some are covered with regular scales. Their colors, including blues and lavenders, appear in many combinations. Like human fingerprints, no two fish are exactly alike. Scaleless fish are dull at first, but begin to color

The common goldfish is just about the ultimate beginner's pond fish. Just remember to stock lightly at first to give your pond a chance to become biologically established.

about the same time as the scaled varieties do, and the first patches of color which form stay as long as the fish live.

Comet
The Comet was first reported in the late 1880s in the ponds of the Fish Commission, in Washington, D.C. It is truly an American fish. The body is more elongated, with much more elaborate fin and tail development than the common goldfish, from which it descended. The extensive fins and tail make the Comet the most streamlined of all goldfish. While typically all gold, the

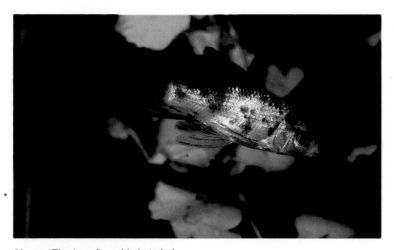

Above: *The long-finned koi strain is an exciting new development in the fish breeder's craft. The fish shown above is very young and will likely develop more color as it matures.*

Below: *The comet goldfish is a time-honored pond inhabitant cherished for its color and active nature.*

Comet may also have markings of white and/or black. It is very hardy.

Shubunkin

The Shubunkin's form and size resemble the Comet, but its coloring is different. Blue is particularly prized in the Shubunkin. It is often the base color over which patches of red, gold, black, and darker blue are laid. Usually there are two or more colors on a fish. The Shubunkin was developed by the Japanese at the beginning of the 20th century. Like the Comet, it is hardy and quite active.

Japanese Fantail and Calico Fantail

The Japanese Fantail and Calico Fantail are beautiful additions to any pool. They differ from the Comet with their refined and gracefully rounded body shape. Their doubled tails and fins are longer and more flowing than are

the Comet's. They swim with a slow, stately and formal manner, which makes them a pleasure to observe. The Japanese Fantail is distinguished by its golden-orange color, sometimes with splashes of white or black. Rarer still is the pearly-white Japanese Fantail. Although a few show this color while young, it is more often observed in mature fish, especially if fed a high (40%) protein diet. Don't be disturbed if your gold Fantail or Comet turns pearly-white. The fish is still healthy. The Calico Fantail, like its namesake, is multicolored with patches of blue, black, red, white, and gold.

Oranda

At first glance, the Oranda looks like a Japanese Fantail. But a closer examination reveals a more esthetically pleasing fish. Years of breeding developed a more compact body shape, longer tail and fins, balanced by

American Shubunkin.

Above: *Fantail varieties are very popular pond fish because of their long, flowing double tails and gracefully rounded bodies.*

Below: *Black Moor telescope-eyed goldfish offer beauty, interest, and variety to any fish pond.*

a dainty cap on its head. The Oranda is a more delicate fish, and thrives in protected ponds and in warmer weather. If you expect ice to cover your pool for more than two consecutive days, I recommend keeping this variety indoors in an aerated tank.

Black Chinese Moor

Always popular with water gardeners, the Black Chinese Moor has unusual telescopic eyes, a compact body, and long tail and fins. Its velvety-black color compliments the brighter colors of other pool fish. It is a

In Japan, where there is so little space available that a flower garden is an impossible dream for most, people take small areas and 'plant' them with living flowers—koi.

delicate fish, but it can readily survive when proper winter care procedures are followed.

Golden Orfe *(Leuciscus idus)*

Highly valued for its speed, constant movement, and surface swimming characteristics, the Golden Orfe is an exciting addition to a pool. Stock your pool with more than one Orfe so that you can observe them swimming together. They are schooling fish. As a member of the trout family, the Golden Orfe jumps above the water in pursuit of insects. Because of this, it should not be put in a pool whose rim would prevent it from flipping back into the water. However, unlike the trout, the Golden Orfe is a peaceful fish, compatible with goldfish and koi.

The red telescope oranda.

The red crucian carp.

A long-tailed crucian carp.

Its long streamlined body is shaped like a torpedo. Contrasted with the red orange tint of goldfish, the Golden Orfe's color more closely resembles a silvery orange. This makes it a brilliant, flashy fish when sunlight hits it. It is sensitive to some chemicals, and caution should be used before adding chemicals to your pool. Your aquatic dealer can recommend appropriate products to be used with Orfes.

Koi *(Cyprinus carpio)*
Just as *Victoria* is the queen of the water lilies, koi is the king of the pool fish. No fish is more striking. Its gentle nature, vibrant colors, enormous potential size, long life, and spectacular patterns have made the koi the favorite pet of Japan. koi are bred in a dazzling variety of colors and patterns. Blue, white, red, black, gold, silver, orange, and copper are some of the available colors.

Like a goldfish, a koi grows according to the size of its pool, but far surpasses a goldfish in size, reaching up to three or four feet in length. Its life span may be 70 years, but koi have been reported to live for over 100 years. Japanese owners pass their beloved koi from generation to generation.

Koi which are bred in Japan are, in general, superior in

These long-finned koi are very new developments in fishkeeping. After the finnage is established, it will be possible to introduce all the colors koi are noted for, resulting in truly fantastic fish with flowing fins, impressive size, and gorgeous colors.

Above: *At a certain age, almost all silver orfe metamorphose into golden orfe.*

Below: *A golden orfe prepares to dine on a Zebra Butterfly.*

Children love to feed the friendly koi in a garden pond. Adult supervision to prevent accidents is highly recommended.

quality to koi bred in America. The Japanese have a much keener interest in and love of koi, dating from centuries ago. However, the gap is narrowing. From every million fry (baby fish), only a few hundred are selected as worthy koi. Of those few, with luck, one fish will become a grand champion.

Because koi are considered a symbol of masculinity in Japan, every year on Boy's Day, May 5, a koi banner is flown for every male in the house. Yet it is a female koi which consistently wins grand champion awards, often because of her more rounded body shape and larger size.

koi love to root in the mud. Gravel over soil in your planting container may discourage small koi under eight inches from muddying your pool and dislodging your plants. With larger koi I recommend a protective screen, through which plants can grow, be placed over your soil containers. I also recommend starting plants in a pool without koi over eight inches, then transferring them,

147

with protective screens, to the koi pond when they are established.

Sometimes protection isn't needed, as is the case at the U.S. National Arboretum in Washington, D.C. At the Arboretum each summer in a moat that surrounds the administration building there is a splendid display of water lilies and lotus. And swimming among them are beautiful giant koi, which do not hinder the plant display.

INTRODUCING YOUR FISH TO THEIR NEW HOME

Fish are typically transported from the dealer in an oxygen-inflated polyethylene bag. Ideally, you should have an isolation pool to serve as a temporary home for your new fish for about

Mirror carp. Through breeding, the scales have been almost totally eliminated.

ten days, so that you can see if they carry any pathogens which might cause health problems. If infected, the new arrivals can be treated without exposing your old stock to the pathogens.

If the fish are gasping while in the bag, release them into the isolation pool as quickly as possible. Otherwise float the bag on the pool surface for 10 to 15 minutes, so that the water in the bag can gradually equal your pool's water temperature. Fish can withstand a wide range of temperatures, but sudden temperature change can cause shock. Place a towel over the floating bag when the sun is shining, to prevent a greenhouse-effect heat problem.

While the bag is floating on your pond's surface, it is a good time to add a preventative broad-spectrum treatment to the isolation pool. Argucide *or* Desa Fin *and* Terramycin *and* a pound of rock salt per 100 gallons are

The original home of the common carp was Asia, but today it is distributed throughout Europe as well. One caveat for the responsible fishkeeper: Please never, never release your fish into natural waterways—the results could be devastating to the ecological balance for years to come.

what I recommend. This three-pronged treatment can prevent later heartache. Also add chlorine – removing agent to remove chlorine, chlorine dioxide, or chloramine if one of

these is in your pool water.

Now carefully open the bag, using a knife if needed, and gently pour the fish and the entire contents into your pool.

FEEDING YOUR FISH

Usually, the most enjoyable aspect of keeping fish is feeding them. By feeding your fish a good quality floating food, you can easily view your fish. Select a well-prepared food, balanced for goldfish and koi. The protein content should not exceed 40%.

You may supplement your fish's diet with finely chopped lettuce, or some other vegetable, such as green peas.

Your fish naturally eat algae, submerged plants, and insects, helping them to achieve a well-balanced diet. Do not feed fish oatmeal, since it is high in carbohydrates and contains very little protein. It is better not to feed your fish anything rather than to feed them a diet of oatmeal.

Spirulina, an algae, has been proven to enhance the colors of goldfish and koi. By feeding your fish prepared food which contains *Spirulina,* you will notice an added vibrancy to their colors. It may take three to four weeks before you see a difference. Reds and blacks are especially responsive to *Spirulina.*

Feed your fish what they can eat in 10 minutes, once or twice a day. Scoop out any excess fish food before it falls to the bottom of the pool and decays. You will soon learn the amount of food to feed your fish. In time, you can even teach them to take food from your hand. Discontinue feeding when the water temperature drops below 45°.

In winter, a dangerous factor in the snowbelt is ice covering your pool. Danger develops from ice coverage, even thin ice coverage, because it blocks the

Feeding your fish will be as much fun for you as them. Enjoy feeding your fish a variety of nutritious foods.

Pseudemys scripta elegans, *red-eared slider turtles are visitors to many ponds. Turtles do not eat water lilies, but they are notorious for snapping off the stems. Occasionally, they may snare a small fish, but they are not particularly fast or adept at fishing.*

water's contact with the atmosphere. Without ice, carbon dioxide from the fish and gases from decaying organic matter (such as leaves) escape from the water into the atmosphere, and are replaced by oxygen. When ice remains too long, this process cannot take place and your fish may suffocate.

Some water gardeners cover their pools with canvas or polyethylene that is placed over beams. The covering may have leaves over it for extra insulation. Be sure to always allow an opening, away from the coldest wind, for needed air exchange.

A favorite way to protect fish is to use a pool de-icer. It is powered by the same outlet that

One way to encourage spawning in your pond fish is to increase the amount of live foods in the diet.

your pump uses. A thermostat automatically turns the heating element on and off as needed. For in-ground ponds which are threatened by more than five consecutive days of ice, I suggest using a 1000-watt unit. If your pool is partially or entirely above ground or gets greater ice coverage, you will need even more protection.

If you are in doubt about your fish's safety outdoors during winter's cold, you may keep them in a tank in the basement or in a heated garage. Temperatures in the 50s are fine. Use an air pump, and your typical garden pool fish assortment should have plenty of oxygen when allowed a gallon of water per inch of fish length. (Like most general rules, this won't work in every case. For example, it would not be safe for

A school of koi enjoying their ration of pellets.

keeping one 20-inch koi in a 20-gallon container. It is meant for a typical garden pool assortment of ornamental fish.)

Cover the tank with a screen to prevent fish from jumping out, especially if you have koi or Golden Orfes. Return the fish to. your pond after the possibility of 24-hour ice cover has safely passed. Remember to slowly adjust water temperature to avoid temperature shock. It's a good idea to blend some pool water into the tank water to help fish gradually adjust to their new water conditions.

SCAVENGERS

Scavengers play a role in maintaining a healthy balanced garden pool. I find the best ones are Japanese Snails, *Viviparus malleatus*. These snails bear living miniatures of themselves one to three times during the growing season. Adults grow to be slightly larger than one inch in diameter. They quietly perform their sanitation department chores, eating leftover fish food and dead leaves. They also graze on the beneficial moss-like algae growing on the pool walls. Japanese Snails do not harm any plant in or out of the pool, nor do they venture out of water. These snails do not overpopulate either, and somehow maintain a proper population level. I suggest for most garden pools that you stock one Japanese Snail for each square foot of surface area.

Tadpoles and frogs are for those who simply must have these delightful creatures. Tadpoles eat fish food and moss-like algae. Frogs thrive on insects. They have been known to eat fish and other small animals as well. I know water gardeners whose main purpose in having a pond is to maintain a proper environment for their pet frogs. Yes, they lose a fish now and then, but nature replenishes the fish population each spring. The pool balance is maintained by itself. Frogs give a concert every summer evening. There is

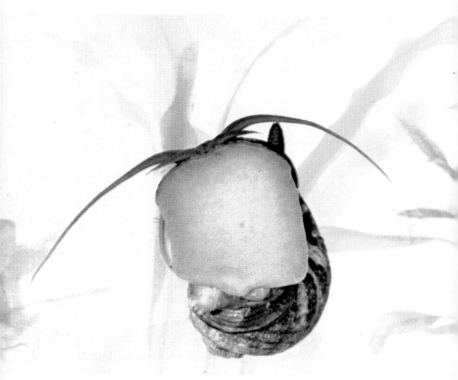

Snails are useful scavengers in ponds as long as they don't overpopulate.

no guarantee that they will stay in your pool. Access to a dry place (a lily pad does nicely) is essential. They bury themselves in mud in advance of freezing weather.

Others have water gardens for pet turtles. While they prefer non-living food, they sometimes snap in half the stem of a water lily pad or blossom. If especially hungry, they may even consume a fish. They are most happy with table scraps. They must be provided with access to a dry

area so they can sun themselves. Otherwise, they develop skin fungus. Like frogs, they may roam, especially during rainy weather.

WATER QUALITY

The most important factor in maintaining your ornamental fish is water quality. Harsh chemicals such as chlorine, chlorine dioxide, and chloramine must be removed. Toxic levels of ammonia and nitrite must be avoided. Proper pH is also essential. By taking simple precautions when you first establish your pond, many problems may be avoided. Inexpensive test kits enable you to monitor your water. A telephone call to your local water department will let you know if chlorine, chloramine, or chlorine dioxide is being added to your water treatment system. Your local aquarium shop has test kits

Newts and salamanders are frequent visitors and even permanent residents of outdoor garden ponds.

to measure necessary water conditions.

Chlorine has been added to drinking water for so many years that almost everyone is aware of its danger to fish. With chlorine, you can let water stand for a few days and the chlorine is gone. But in many areas, chlorine has been replaced. New chemicals, chloramine and chlorine dioxide, are being added daily to many

water treatment systems. These chemicals are very stable and do not quickly dissipate from standing water into the atmosphere, as chlorine does. It is therefore very important to use a treatment such as DeChlor or Aqua Safe to neutralize the toxic effects of these chemicals whenever tap water from a community water system is added to your pool.

Chloramine

Chloramine has become increasingly familiar to fish keepers. This chlorine and ammonia compound is extremely

dangerous to your fish, even more so than chlorine. Fish react to chloramine poisoning differently than they do to chlorine poisoning. Chlorine burns a fish's gills, causing it to suffocate due to its inability to utilize dissolved oxygen. Characteristically, affected fish are seen in a stressed condition, gulping at the surface.

Chloramine, on the other hand, passes through the gill membrane and enters the blood stream. Therefore, upon initial exposure, the fish do not appear stressed. In simple terms, chloramine breaks down red blood cells. General symptoms appear a few days after the

A frog rests on the buoyant leaf of the Gloriosa lily.

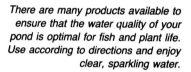

There are many products available to ensure that the water quality of your pond is optimal for fish and plant life. Use according to directions and enjoy clear, sparkling water.

poisoning, but often too late to save the fish. These include hiding, not eating, and listless behavior. In the last stages, fish gasp at the surface and eventually die.

pH, Ammonia and Nitrite

Acidity and alkalinity of water are measured in terms of pH. An ideal range for ornamental pool fish is 6.8 to 7.4. Readings of 7.0 are neutral. Anything below 7.0 indicates an acid condition, while readings above 7.0 show alkalinity. The pH value may be adjusted by using water quality control products. Your local pet shop sells many types. While goldfish can live in a much wider pH range, the wider range water chemistry is much less stable than the ideal range. With a high

pH, active ammonia ions are in the water, so a dangerous ammonia level may develop. With a pH of 7.0, there is virtually no free ammonia in the water.

Organic waste materials (leaves, fish waste, leftover fish food) are broken down into ammonia by bacteria. The ammonia transforms into nitrite and is finally broken down to nitrate, which is harmless. Normally, the organic matter is broken down so quickly that there isn't a problem. Bacteria cause organic material to form ammonia, then nitrite, then nitrate.

When a pool is overloaded with organic matter, high ammonia levels often occur. High ammonia also develops in clean new pools and thoroughly cleaned old pools. The reason is a lack of the required nitrifying bacteria. In addition, there is a tendency for beginners to overfeed fish at first. This leads to too much decomposing fish food and fish waste, which can contribute to the ammonia problem. It is best to allow your pool water to age for a few weeks in a new or completely cleaned old pool prior to stocking with valuable fish. Otherwise, a product such as Aqua Safe or Clear Pond may be added. Be sure to monitor the pH and ammonia levels daily for the first weeks. If the pH level alone is controlled, a potential ammonia problem can be avoided.

The information in the previous

The water quality of your pond will make a big difference between success and failure. A small investment in a water test kit at the outset will help you provide the best water for your stock.

paragraph shows why experienced water gardeners do not remove the beneficial moss-like algae growing on the pool sides. If it is necessary to drain the pool to remove an accumulation of debris, this is fine. But, don't remove the moss-like algae since it will help to balance your pool. This helpful algae is also an auxiliary food source for your fish.

CLEAR WATER

Naturally balancing a pond and achieving clear water can be quite simple as long as you have a good supply of patience. It may take six to eight weeks for your pool to settle, but it will settle as long as you don't change the water. Add one bunch of submerged plants per one to two square feet of surface, one scavenger per surface square foot, and enough water lilies to shade at least half of the water surface.

Submerged plants are the

Green Smoke.

Clear water reflects sky and marginal flowers beautifully, as well as providing good view of your fish.

most important factor in maintaining clear water. They starve algae by absorbing the carbon dioxide and mineral salts essential for algal growth. Water lilies help, too. As their pads grow, their shade impedes unwanted algal growth.

Scavengers graze on the moss-like algae which grow on the sides of pools, leftover fish food, and fish waste. Overfeeding your fish will contribute to algae growth,

unsafe ammonia levels, and unhappy fish. Feed them what they will eat in 10 minutes, once or twice a day. Reducing the amount of daily fish food can sometimes help an overly green pond become less green.

Please remember that your pond can be in balance without clear water. In fact, fish thrive in green water of the intensity whereby you can barely see your hand when submerged a foot into the water. If this degree of opacity is acceptable, you don't need a filter. Moreover, you may only need about a third of the guideline suggestions for snails and submerged plants. However, if you prefer your fish to be more visible or if you simply prefer clear, or nearly clear water, then follow the guidelines. You may want a filter to use while waiting for the plants and scavengers to get started initially, and early in the season before the submerged plants become effective.

The green of this water is a reflection of plants and trees, not over-abundant algal growth, as evidenced by the clear view of the fish below the water's surface.

FILTERS

You can add a pool filter to speed along the process of balancing a pond. It is a great timesaver. A filter traps fish wastes, sediments, algae and other suspended matter. Because a filter is so efficient in removing suspended matter, your pond is less likely to become cloudy. The more frequently water passes through the filter media, the more suspended matter is removed. With a mechanical filter, circulation is most important.

Aim for circulating the entire volume of pond water through

the filter approximately once every two hours. For example, a pond holding 400 gallons needs a filter with a pump that has a capacity of at least 200 gallons per hour. If you are using the filter's pump to run water through a waterfall, statuary, or fountain, you may have to choose a larger pump for adequate circulation. The reason is that lifting water to any one of these features puts back-pressure on the pump, slowing it. The resulting drop in circulation could make the

Fancy fish like the telescope-eyed goldfish peeking out of the water here have space to develop fully in a protected pond.

filtering system inadequate. Fountains put so much back-pressure against pumps that I recommend using a separate pump for them.

DETERMINING NUMBER OF GALLONS

To accurately determine the number of gallons in your pool, accurate measurements are necessary. For a rectangle, multiply length times width times depth (all in feet) to determine the number of cubic feet. For a circle, multiply radius times radius times 3.14 times depth for the number of cubic feet. There are 7.5 gallons of water per cubic foot. Therefore, multiply 7.5 times the number of cubic

The attractive red salamander, Pseudotriton reber schnecki, is apt to be a visitor at the pond. For most people, the visiting wildlife to even the smallest garden pond is an additional benefit.

feet to find the number of gallons.

These formulas assume that there are vertical sides and level bottoms. Sloping sides reduce gallonage, as do objects in the pool, and the pool being less than full. In irregular ponds, approximate the number of gallons by making imaginary shapes (rectangles, circles, half circles) out of it and then adding their respective numbers to reach a total.

STRESS

Fish carry pathogens which cause no problem until the fish are stressed. A number of factors cause stress, including oxygen depletion, spawning, sudden temperature changes, improper pH, and handling. Once fish are stressed, they become more susceptible to pathogens.

If you can't pinpoint the problem, treat the pond with a combination of rock salt (kosher salt, ice cream salt) or consult your pet shop staff for the proper remedy and dosage. Do not mix medications in other combinations unadvisedly. The result could be fatalities.

Rock salt is a good temporary

Is there anyone who doesn't enjoy a fountain? Even the ancient Romans appreciated the beauty of fountains, as evidenced by the presence of centuries-old fountains in virtually every country occupied by the Roman Empire.

treatment for restoring vigor to fish. One pound of rock salt treats 100 gallons. Rock salt helps your fish restore their protective slime layer and electrolytes. Be sure to pre-mix medications with pool water before adding them to the pool.

OVERCROWDING

Overcrowding the pond with fish can cause stress. Natural increase in number and size of fish or the unwise addition of fish may cause a pool to be overcrowded. This may result in stress through the lack of sufficient oxygen.

Your pool obtains oxygen directly from the atmosphere and, during hours of sunlight, from submerged green plants. Keep in mind that as water becomes warmer it holds less oxygen.

Fish, being cold-blooded, increase their body temperature as water warms. As fish become warmer, their body processes speed up, requiring more oxygen; so that when they need more oxygen, less is available. This is why you must be especially alert during the hottest time of the year for a low oxygen situation.

At night, plants consume oxygen and give off carbon dioxide. Therefore, the lowest oxygen level in your pool usually occurs during the last hour of darkness.

Fish that are low on oxygen slowly work their mouths at the water's surface, gasping for relief. Remedies include reducing the fish population, using an air

Koi schooling in circles in a beautiful Japanese pond.

pump, operating a fountain or waterfall to aerate the water. Temporary relief is available by adding a spray of water from the garden hose. Remember to treat the new water if it contains chlorine, chloramine, or chlorine dioxide.

BREEDING

Goldfish and koi usually spawn in the spring or sometimes in the fall, especially when water temperatures are between 55° and 60°. The female, her body swollen with eggs, swims rapidly over a spawning mat or over and through leaf masses of submerged plants, rubbing against them as she goes and depositing perhaps several hundred eggs. Eggs are pale amber gray, about the size of pinheads.

A male goldfish can be distinguished during the breeding season by the series of white dots (tubercles) which appear along the side of gill plates and along the leading edge of his front fins. Males can be seen scurrying after a female, to fertilize the eggs as she lays them. This process—a female vigorously swimming about laying eggs, and three or four males in pursuit—is the well-known fish circus which can often be observed. The circus usually begins early in the morning and lasts until around noon. If you have breeding size goldfish (over three inches) or breeding size koi (at least 8 to 10

HATCHING

Goldfish and koi eggs hatch in three to seven days, depending upon the water temperature. Cool water delays hatching. Silver-gray fry emerge head up. Within 24 hours, a fry's swim bladder will have gained the tiny amount of air required for

The spawning chase of the goldfish culminates in several hundred fry—natural regeneration of your fish stock.

inches), be sure to provide a spawning mat or submerged plants for spawning. Otherwise, the female may literally be chased to death while desperately searching in vain for a proper place to deposit her eggs.

horizontal swimming. Some begin to show color in six weeks, under ideal circumstances. Feed the fry crumbled flake food and basically just leave them alone. The fewer handlings, the better off they are.

Most of the eggs and fry are eaten if left in the pond, so if you have more than one pond, use a spawning mat. Once the eggs are laid on the mat, transfer them to a pool without fish.

166

Another method is to make a nursery where the eggs can hatch and the fry can grow to an inch and a half in size. They can then fend for themselves. What you do is to suspend a fine-meshed basket into your pond. This will give the eggs and fry a pool environment that is safe from the predation of other fish. If you do nothing to protect the eggs and fry, you may realize a gain of a dozen or two dozen fish from hundreds or thousands of eggs. Do not worry about overpopulation. Your fish will multiply in relation to the space and food available for them. When they reach that point, few or no baby fish will be added. Then, should a disaster strike and you lose a lot of fish, expect a significant natural increase to occur the following spring. Ah, the wonders of nature!

Hatching goldfish eggs. Some fry pop out of the egg as sticky little fish while others just have their tails protruding through the egg case.

PREDATORS OF ORNAMENTAL FISH

Predators of ornamental fish include raccoons, catfish and other wild fish, fish-eating birds, cats, water snakes, turtles, and frogs. Sometimes, though, you can end up with so many fish that you can share your surplus with friends.

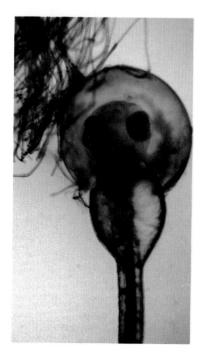

Close-up of goldfish fry about to hatch. Within minutes he will wriggle free of his egg case and begin the adventure of life.

167

The marginal plants bordering this water garden soften and accent the rocky edges.

King of the Blues.

Accessory Aquatic Plants

The balance of life in a water garden is strong and natural, seldom requiring any adjustment it cannot make for itself. At the same time, it is intricate and interdependent. Successful water gardeners use a combination of water lilies (lotus sometimes), ornamental fish, scavengers, and accessory plants.

There seems to be no limit to the number of accessory plants, so I am including here only those that are available from major aquatic plant specialists. And I exclude those that are illegal to possess in some states or illegal to ship in interstate commerce. Such plants, including water hyacinths, are considered dangerous to the environment because they multiply rapidly at the expense of other plants and can clog waterways.

The banana plant blooms readily under most pond conditions.

SUBMERGED PLANTS—CLEAR WATER

There are certain aquatic plants that can help keep pool water clear or nearly clear. These are submerged plants like *Anacharis, Cabomba,* and *Myriophyllum.* They are often misleadingly referred to as **oxygenating** plants. I say misleadingly because this descriptive term is true of green plants as a whole, not just of submerged plants. Moreover, this term is misleading because it implies that these plants provide extra oxygen 24 hours a day. While it is true that by the process of photosynthesis they do provide oxygen in the presence of sunlight, this is not the whole story. Plants respire—use oxygen and release carbon dioxide—24 hours a day. They photosynthesize—release oxygen and use carbon dioxide—only in the presence of sunlight. The net gain in oxygen during a 24 hour period is minimal.

Above: *The stately Bog Arum,* Calla palustris, *in full bloom is an unforgettable sight.*

Still, these submerged plants are desirable, because they serve as a spawning medium for your fish and render a valuable service when stocked in sufficient numbers. Their foliage competes with algae for nutrients from the water. If you stock one bunch (six stems) of submerged plants for every one or two square feet of water surface, they do a good job at keeping your pool water clear or nearly clear. Allow at least six weeks for the process to take

Below: *Masses of the small yellow flowers of the Marsh Marigold are sure to brighten anyone's day.*

effect. If you begin in mid-summer when you can barely see down through six inches of water, they may need at least twice as much time to be effective. I'm assuming that your pool includes a balance of water

Double Flowering Arrowhead presents absolutely incredible full white flowers.

lilies, accessory aquatic plants, ornamental fish, and scavengers.

Submerged plants are usually purchased as cuttings. Pot them in a heavy garden top soil, after first removing the rubber band from the bunch, and press the stems one to two inches into the soil. Top it off with pea gravel as you do with water lilies. Grow them in water over six inches

The semi-aquatic irises blend well along pool margins.

deep. If your pool water is green or cloudy, be sure that at least the tops of the stems are close enough to the water surface to benefit from the required sunlight. If your fish are over six inches long, allow newly potted submerged plants to become established in another pool before allowing these fish to nibble at them. Or, you may cover the new plantings with a dome of chicken wire or you can purchase a protective device from your aquatic plant dealer.

MARGINAL AQUATIC PLANTS
Marginal aquatic plants soften the line where pond and earth meet, and also provide a varied setting for your water lilies, making your pond a more beautiful place in general. Even in a formal pool, it is a good idea to plant the corners and the center with a variety of graceful marginal plants.

Grow your marginal plants at a water depth of zero to 12 inches. Zero means the soil is saturated with water.

Using a soil container at least four inches deep and having a surface area equal to the size you want your planting to cover in your pond, fill it with heavy garden top soil. Add water lily fertilizer at one half of the rate the label recommends for water

Henry Shaw

Louella G. Uber.

satisfactory for Anacharis, Cabomba, Myriophyllum, and Vallisneria. Dwarf Sagittaria performs well in full or partial sun. Summer is blooming season for Dwarf Sagittaria, Myriophyllum, Cabomba, and Anacharis. Water depth is 6 to 30 inches for Anacharis, Cabomba, Myriophyllum, and Dwarf Sagittaria. Water depth for Vallisneria is 6 to 24 inches.

HARDY BOG PLANTS

Arrowhead is a distinctively foliaged plant, producing

attractive three-petaled white flowers. Height, 24 inches. Full or partial sun. Summer blooming season. **Double Flowering Arrowhead** produces very attractive double white flowers. Height, 24 inches. Full or partial sun. Summer blooming. **Water Arum** has glossy, arrowhead-shaped leaves and yellow-green flowers. Height, 24 inches. Full or partial sun. Summer blooming. **Dwarf Bamboo** is excellent for low screening or borders, not overly invasive. Flowers are insignificant, produces club-like structures. Height, 18 inches. Full or partial

Flower of Cabomba australis.

Forget-Me-Nots, Myosotis.

sun. Summer blooming. **Bog Bean** is an excellent plant for masking pool edges. Creeping habit. White flowers. Height, 12 inches. Partial or filtered sun. Spring blooming. **White Bullrush** is a good accent plant with tall, 4 to 6 foot, cylindrical, nearly white leaves. Full or partial sun. Summer blooming. **Thalia** produces tall, graceful, purple-flowering stems held well above the bold, 3 to 4 foot foliage. Height, 6 feet. Blooms in full or partial sun in summer. **Cattail** is a tall plant, 7 feet high, good for accent or screening. Invasive in earthen ponds. Shorter in containers. Full or partial sun; summer blooming. **Graceful Cattail** delivers graceful, 4 feet high, narrow leaves. Good background or

Flower of Cabomba pulcherima.

screening plant. Full or partial sun; late summer to fall blooming season. **Dwarf Cattail** is a short cattail, 24 inches high, with very graceful leaves that are excellent for low screening. Full or partial sun. Late summer to fall blooming. **Narrow-Leaved Cattail** has graceful leaves that are very attractive swaying in a breeze. Seven feet tall. Invasive in earthen ponds, shorter in containers. Full or partial sun. Summer blooming. **Chinese Water Chestnut** has graceful, cylindrical stems and grows to a

sunlight. Spring to early summer blooming season. **Horsetail** has a club-like structure with jointed stems. Grows to 3 feet. Full or partial sun. Summer to fall bloomer. **Lizard's Tail** has fragrant white flowers produced on long spikes. Grows to 18 inches. Full or partial sun. Summer blooming season. Leaves are somewhat heart-shaped. **Parrot's Feather** is grown for its lime green foliage which trails along the surface of the water. Stems sometimes held slightly above the surface.

Water Poppy, Limnocharis humboldti.

height of 3 feet. Produces tuber used in oriental cooking. Blooms in summer to fall. Full or partial sun. **Floating Heart** has five-petaled yellow flowers held slightly above water surface. Three-inch green and maroon variegated leaves. Full or partial sun. Blooming season is spring to fall. **Golden Club** has white spikes tipped with brilliant yellow. Grows to one foot. Partial

Good for spawning. Full or partial sun. **Flowering Rush** produces three-petaled pink flowers borne in graceful clusters. **Pickerel Rush** is an excellent clumping plant with purple spike flowers. Grows to 3 feet. Full sun. Mid-summer blooming season. **White Pickerel Rush** is the white form of the Pickerel Rush. Grows to 30 inches. Full or partial sun. Spring to early fall blooming season.

White Water Snowflake, **Nymphoides indicum.**

Spike Rush is a low border plant, excellent in bogs. Club-like light brown flower structure on narrow, quill-shaped leaves. Grows to 12 inches. Full or partial sun. Summer to fall blooming season. **Sagittaria** bears tiny white flowers and the leaves are bright green and grass-like. Grows to 24 inches. Full, partial or filtered light. Early spring to fall blooming season. **Yellow Snowflake** has bright yellow flowers with chocolate brown leaves patterned with green veins. **White Snowflake** species produces fragrant white flowers in abundance. Full or partial sun. Summer to fall blooming season. **Sweetflag** has iris-like leaves that produce a strong, sweet aroma when crushed. Grows to 30 inches. Full or partial sun. Summer blooming season. **Four Leaf Water Clover** has leaves marked with a beautiful brown to yellow pattern. Full, partial, or filtered sun.

The Yellow Snowflake, White Snowflake, Floating Heart, Parrot's Feather, and Four Leaf Water Clover are floating plants with roots in soil. The remainder of the above-mentioned plants are upright in their growth habits and of varying heights. The water depth for planting is also variable as follows, with "0" representing bog or wet soil: 0-2 inches— Spike Rush; 0-4 inches—Dwarf Bamboo and Bog Bean; 0-6 inches—Golden Club, Horsetail, Lizard's Tail, Flowering Rush, Sweetflag, Arrowhead, Water Arum, White Bullrush, Graceful Cattail, Dwarf Cattail; 0-7 inches—Double Flowering Arrowhead; 0-12 inches— Pickerel Rush, Sagittaria, Thalia, Cattail, Narrow Leaved Cattail, and Chinese Water Chestnut; 4-12 inches—Floating Heart, Parrot's Feather, Yellow Snowflake, White Snowflake, and Four Leaf Water Clover.

TROPICAL BOG PLANTS
Bog Lily is an upright plant that grows to a height of 2 feet. Full or partial sun. Blooming season

Golden Club, Orontium aquaticum.

is summer. The long petaled, white flowers are very fragrant. **Water Canna** grows upright to a height of 4 feet. It requires full sun and has a summer blooming season. Tropical Cannas are adaptable to aquatic environs. Red, yellow, or orange varieties. **Red Stemmed Thalia** is a large, upright plant that reaches a height of 5 feet. Full sun. Summer blooming season. This plant grows in clumps. Bold leaves are supported on red stems. **Dwarf Papyrus** is an upright plant that grows to 30 inches. Tolerating full, partial, or filtered sun, it is a summer-blooming plant. Tufts of wheat-colored foliage are borne atop 24- to 30-inch stems. **Water Poppy** is a floating plant, full or partial sun. Bears three-petaled, yellow flowers that are held slightly above the water's surface. Leaves are nearly round. Summer blooming. **Red Stemmed Sagittaria** is an upright plant, reaching 4 feet in

height. Full sun. Summer blooming. Bold, red stems support flaring green leaves. **Spider Lily**, an upright plant, 2 feet in height. Full or partial sun. Spring to summer blooming. Very narrow petaled, large fragrant white flowers are the outstanding features of this plant. **Green Taro** is an upright, 42 inches tall, with a summer blooming season. Full or partial sun. Grown for distinctively shaped dark green foliage, yellow blooms. Poi is made from tubers of this plant. **Violet Stemmed Taro**, an upright, 42 inches tall. Full or partial sun. Summer blooming. Violet stemmed with lush foliage, yellow flowers. Makes a bold addition to the landscape. **Umbrella Palm** is an upright plant, 5 feet in height. Full, partial, or filtered sun. Summer

Irises grow where the water's edge meets the rise of the soil. They provide interest and variety to your water garden through their variety of colors and height.

blooming. Grown for its distinctive foliage borne in whorls. Good for tall screening or accent.

Water depth: ("0" represents bog or wet soil: 0-6 inches— Bog Lily, Water Canna, Red Stemmed Thalia, Dwarf Papyrus, Red Stemmed Sagittaria, Spider Lily, Umbrella Palm; 0-12 inches— Green Taro, Violet Stemmed Taro; 4-12 inches— Water Poppy.

IRIS

Bayou Comus grows to 24 inches tall. This is a semi-hardy iris with a blooming season of mid to late spring. Full or partial

sun. **Black Gamecock** is a 24-inch plant with rich, blue-black flowers. Full or partial sun. Early to mid-spring blooming. **Blue Iris** has medium blue flowers and reaches a height of 24 inches. Full or partial sun. Blooms early to mid-spring. **Clyde Redmond** reaches a height of 24 inches. Blooms with extremely dark blue flowers in mid-spring. Full or partial sun. **Eolian** reaches a height of 42 inches. Outstanding, large sky-blue flowers make this a magnificent selection. Blooms in full or partial sun during mid to late spring. **Her Highness** reaches a height of 36 inches. Stately, large white flowers on erect stems. Full or partial sun. Early to late spring blooming. **Kaempferi varieties** grow to 30 inches. Large petaled flowers, sold as mixed colors with blue, purple, and white. Plant in boggy areas that are not flooded in winter. Fertilize lightly in early spring. Full sun. Blooms early to mid-summer. **Katherine Cornay** grows to 36 inches. Full or partial sun. Blooms mid to late spring. Semi-hardy iris produces large lavender flowers on erect stems. **Marie Caillet** grows to 36 inches. Full or partial sun. Large orchid purple flowers are held on stately stems. Blooms mid to late spring. **Mistis** grows to 36 inches. Full or partial sun. Blooms mid-spring. Regal, violet

This lovely white iris with a yellow throat will stand proud and hold its head high next to any other flower in your water garden.

Iris versicolor, *Blue Iris, will awaken your water garden in the early spring with soft blue flowers and narrow graceful foliage.*

colored iris. Clumps well. Semi-hardy iris. **Red Iris** grows to 24 inches. The thin, narrow leaves give a very graceful appearance. Red blossoms in early to late spring. Full or partial sun. **Siberian Iris** grows to 36 inches. Full or partial sun. Showy, royal purple flowers are outstanding. Bloom in mid to late spring. **Yellow Water Iris** grows to 30 inches. Full sun. Excellent for borders and massing. Blooms early spring. **Double Yellow Water Iris** is a rare, double flowering form of the yellow iris.

Iris prefer a slightly acid soil with some humus. All clump, and can be propagated by root division. Blooming season is earlier in warmer areas, later in cooler areas. All grow upright, height varies.

Water depth: ("0" represents bog or wet soil: 0—Kaempferi varieties; 0-4 inches—Black Gamecock, Double Yellow Water Iris; 0-6 inches—Bayou Comus, Blue Iris, Clyde Redmond, Eolian, Her Highness, Katherine Cornay, Marie Caillet, Mistis, Red Iris; 0-10 inches—Yellow Water Iris.

A beautiful assortment of vividly colored tropical day blooming water lilies.

Ron Watson's stunning indoor pond affords an optimal environment for rare and gorgeous varieties of fish and plant life.

The following is a listing of the scientific and common names of the bog and marginal plants: Floating heart, *Nymphoides peltata*; golden club, *Orontium aquaticum*; horsetail, *Equisetum hymenale*; lizard's tail, *Saururus cernuus*; parrot's feather, *Myriophyllum aquatica*; flowering rush, *Butomus umbellatus*; pickerel rush, *Pontederia cordata*; white pickerel rush, *Pontederia cordata* variety; spike rush, *Eleocharis montevidensis*; yellow snowflake, *Nymphoides geminata*; white snowflake, *Nymphoides cristatum*; sweetflag, *Acorus calamus*; four leaf water clover, *Marsilea mutica*; arrowhead, *Sagittaria latifolia*; double flowering arrowhead, *Sagittaria japonica*; water arum, *Peltandra virginica*; dwarf bamboo, *Dulichium arundinaceum*; bog bean, *Menyanthes trifoliata*; white bullrush, *Scirpus albescens*; thalia, *Thalia dealbata*; cattail, *Typha latifolia*; graceful cattail, *Typha laxmannii*; dwarf cattail, *Typha minima*; narrow leaved cattail, *Typha angustifolia*; Chinese water chestnut, *Eleocharis tuberosa*; iris, *Iris*; bog lily, *Crinum americanum*; water canna, *Canna*; red stemmed thalia, *Thalia geniculata* form *ruminoides*; dwarf papyrus, *Cyperus haspans*; water poppy, *Hydrocleis nymphoides*; red stemmed sagittaria, *Sagittaria lancifolia* form *ruminoides*; spider lily, *Hymenocallis lirisome*; green taro, *Colocasia esculenta*; violet stemmed taro, *Colocasia esculenta* variety *fontanesii*; umbrella palm, *Cyperus alternifolius*.

This exquisite water garden is thoughtfully arranged with walkways—and who knows who you'll meet on your stroll through the water lilies.

Information

Water gardeners have an international plant society available to them, the Water Lily Society. This society is involved with all aspects of water gardening, including aquatic ornamental plants as well as ornamental fish, and how to make them all work together. Each August, the Society holds an annual symposium, preceded and/or followed by two or more days of optional tours of interest to water gardeners. Along with amateur enthusiasts, you can meet water garden writers and lecturers. Within two years of its beginning, September 24, 1984, it had members in 14 countries, 42 U. S. states and the District of Columbia.

A quarterly *Water Garden Journal* is of great interest to society members. For information on the Society, please contact:

Water Lily Society
P. O. Box 104
Buckeystown, Maryland
21717-0104, U.S.A.
(301) 662-2230

If you need information beyond what you find here, I'll be glad to do what I can to give you an answer. Please write to:

Charles B. Thomas
6800 Lilypons Road
P. O. Box 10
Lilypons, Maryland
21717-0010
(301) 874-5133

Suggested Reading

The following books published by T.F.H. Publications are available at pet shops everywhere.

GARDEN PONDS: A COMPLETE INTRODUCTION
By Al David
(T.F.H. CO-017)
This highly colorful book shows and tells readers how to set up, maintain, and keep a garden pond. 114 full color photos and 22 full color line drawings. 96 pages.

GOLDFISH AND KOI IN YOUR HOME
by Dr. Herbert Axelrod
(T.F.H. H-909)
This book contains complete data on the care of goldfish and koi in the home aquarium and garden pond. Contains 208 pages, 91 black and white photos, and 125 color photos.

KOI AND GARDEN PONDS: A COMPLETE INTRODUCTION
By Dr. Herbert R. Axelrod
(T.F.H. CO-040)
For anyone interested in Japanese carp and for owners of garden ponds. Contains 104 full-color photos and 108 full-color line drawings, 96 pages.

KOI OF THE WORLD
by Dr. Herbert R. Axelrod
(T.F.H. H-947)
Koi in your garden—with scores of oversized color photos of types of koi.
Contains 327 color photos, 22 black and white photos, and 239 pages.

GOLDFISH GUIDE
by Dr. Yoshiichi Matsui
(T.F.H. PL-2011)
Written by a foremost Japanese fancier, this book abounds with bedrock information about keeping and breeding goldfish. Illustrated with 100 full-color photos, 256 pages.

Index

188

Page numbers shown in **bold** refer to illustrations.

TS-102

**WATER GARDENS
FOR PLANTS AND FISH**